Playlist

THE REBELS AND REVOLUTIONARIES OF SOUND

James Rhodes

illustrated by Martin O'Neill

CANDLEWICK STUDIO
an imprint of Candlewick Press

CONTENTS

INTRODUCTION

Music. Close your eyes for a moment and just try to imagine a world without it. Can you think of anything more boring, depressing, or lifeless? It would be like living in a black-and-white universe. Music gives flavor and color to the world in which we live. It inspires us, unites us, and can even make us better people. But no matter what music you like, the truth is that it will always have some roots in older music. Because the brand-new music of today was actually born many hundreds of years ago. It has slowly but surely grown, adapted, and evolved to end up with what you hear now at a stadium gig or on Spotify.

I'll be honest with you: classical music is not usually seen as riveting material for a book. I know that. You know that. It is thought of as dull, irrelevant, belonging to other (usually old) people, and about as interesting as algebra. I will say this though: classical music saved my life when I was a kid. And even today, many years later, every single time I listen to it, it makes me feel amazing.

Classical music has a bad and, in my mind, unfair reputation. Those composers with the white curly wigs, such as Bach and Mozart, might seem super-old-fashioned now. But they were the original rock stars. They changed history, inspired millions, and are still listened to and worshipped all around the world today. So I hope you'll leave behind your preconceptions: even if you think you hate it, give it an hour or two of your time and *then* decide.

It does have to be said that there are a LOT of classical composers, and it can be quite overwhelming to decide where to begin. I have chosen seven composers to get us started. For each composer I have selected two pieces to discuss and listen to. I'm also going to explain a bit about the lives of the composers. (You won't believe some of their stories. Did you know Beethoven peed into a chamber pot he kept under his piano and Bach had twenty children?) I've chosen Bach, Mozart, Beethoven, Chopin, Schubert, Rachmaninoff, and Ravel: the perfect introduction to classical music.

You might soon spot that they all look pretty similar, though. Classical music is and has been overwhelmingly white and male. At the time these composers lived, it was much, much easier for men to work—in fact, it was often considered scandalous for women to have a career. And so even though there were super-talented female composers, they didn't receive the financial support and popular recognition they needed to break into the mainstream, nor did they get big opportunities to prove themselves. The same goes for composers of color—despite their obvious gifts, very few of them achieved anything like the success of their white counterparts.

If you want to hear some amazing music from outside the established "classics," try Chevalier de Saint-Georges, known as *le Mozart noir* (the black Mozart). He was born in Guadeloupe to an enslaved mother and a plantation-owner father. He moved to Paris, where he was revealed to be a master fencer and virtuoso violinist. De Saint-Georges composed fourteen violin concertos, six operas, and dozens of chamber works. And he even taught Marie Antoinette the violin! Or search online for Fanny Mendelssohn, who grew up in the shadow of her famous brother, Felix, even publishing some of her work under his name. Then there was Samuel Coleridge-Taylor, a black composer and conductor who studied at London's Royal College of Music and was championed by Edward Elgar. Florence Price was the first black female composer to have a composition performed by a major orchestra (Chicago Symphony in 1933). She wrote three hundred works, many of them drawing on her roots in the American South.

The world of classical music today is slightly more diverse. But the sad truth is that any list of the most significant composers in history will be full of white men, because they were given the means and opportunities to compose and, at least sometimes, succeed. I believe that in another hundred years, that list will be much more inclusive. But, to our collective shame, we will have had a very long wait.

Classical music can seem a bit daunting if you don't understand what words like *symphony* and *étude* mean. So throughout the book I've put in a few sections explaining musical terminology (words that are underlined in the text are defined in the Language of Music glossary), how an orchestra works, and the major styles of classical music. By the end, you will be equipped to go out and discover even more incredible pieces. If you get confused by anything, that will no doubt be my fault. But there is a wealth of information to be found online. Or, if you prefer, ask an adult to tweet me for some answers.

So, this is my plea: give this music a chance. Read the book, listen to the pieces in the playlist I've built for you (turn the page!), and then, if you want, NEVER listen to it again, safe in the knowledge you've given it a go and hated it. But maybe, just maybe, it'll blow your mind and improve your life a little bit, and you'll want to send me a giant box of cookies as a thank-you. (I'm not even joking—send as many as you like.)

Enjoy. Take it slowly. Allow yourself to experience something magical.

James x

MY ULTIMATE PLAYLIST

Before we get started, find the Spotify playlist I've curated for you (or, if you're not old enough to have your own Spotify account, ask someone who has one to help you). Because there is ABSOLUTELY NO POINT just reading a book about classical music—music is there to be listened to. Together, we'll explore these incredible pieces and marvel at the composers who wrote them—not to mention the insanely talented musicians who play them.

The playlist can be accessed through any internet browser using the following link:

tinyurl.com/jamesrhodesplaylist

TITLE	COMPOSER	PERFORMER
Cello Suite No. 1 in G Major, Prelude	Johann Sebastian Bach	Pablo Casals
Goldberg Variations, Aria	Johann Sebastian Bach	Glenn Gould
Requiem in D Minor, Dies Irae	Wolfgang Amadeus Mozart	Musica Aeterna, Teodor Currentzis & The New Siberian Singers
The Marriage of Figaro, Overture	Wolfgang Amadeus Mozart	Teodor Currentzis, Musica Aeterna
'Emperor' Concerto, Second movement	Ludwig van Beethoven	Hélène Grimaud, Staatskapelle Dresden & Vladimir Jurowski
'Eroica' Symphony, First movement	Ludwig van Beethoven	Jordi Savall & Le Concert Des Nations
Étude Op. 10/1 in C Major	Frédéric Chopin	Zlata Chochieva
Nocturne No. 2 in E flat Major	Frédéric Chopin	Fazıl Say
'Ave Maria'	Franz Schubert	Rosmarie Kalin, Alexandra Berving-Wassen, Stella Chamber Choir & Solvieg Agren
Piano Trio No. 2 in E flat Major, Finale	Franz Schubert	Renaud Capuçon, Frank Braley & Gautier Capuçon
Piano Concerto No. 2 in C Minor, Finale	Sergei Rachmaninoff	Valentina Lisitsa, London Symphony Orchestra & Michael Francis
Prelude in G Minor	Sergei Rachmaninoff	Xiayin Wang
Boléro	Maurice Ravel	Boston Symphony Orchestra & Seiji Ozawa
Le Tombeau de Couperin, Toccata	Maurice Ravel	James Rhodes

Found it? Let's dive into the music.

THE FACTS OF LIFE

FULL NAME
Johann Sebastian Bach

BORN
March 21, 1685, Eisenach, Germany

DIED
July 28, 1750, Leipzig, Germany

CAUSE OF DEATH
A stroke following eye surgery

They said:

"I WOULD VOTE FOR BACH, ALL OF BACH, STREAMED OUT INTO SPACE, OVER AND OVER AGAIN. WE WOULD BE BRAGGING OF COURSE."

Lewis Thomas, *author and physician, on what message we should send to an extraterrestrial civilization*

FAMILY AFFAIRS
Bach came from a huge musical family—his grandfather, great-grandfather, uncles, cousins, nephews, and later his own sons were all musicians. Sadly, little Johann's world was filled with death and unhappiness. He lost his father, his mother, and two siblings before he was ten. In later life, Bach went on to have twenty children (and you think having one or two siblings is annoying), but ten of them died at birth or in infancy. And then his first wife, the great love of his life, also died, quite unexpectedly, while Bach was away on business with his boss. Not a very happy life story so far, huh?

MUSICAL OUTPUT
Bach wrote over a thousand **compositions** that we know of today. Even more were composed, but have since been lost. His musical output was vast—roughly the equivalent of 142 albums. To put this in context, that's about seven times the output (so far) of Justin Bieber, Kanye West, and Rihanna *combined*.

BACH-TRACKS
The Beatles ("All You Need Is Love"), Eminem ("Brainless"), Led Zeppelin ("Heartbreaker"), Zayn Malik ("Blue"), Lady Gaga ("Bad Romance"), and Clean Bandit ("A + E") have all referenced or sampled Bach's music.

ON-SCREEN
Bach's music has been used in the soundtracks for *Doctor Who*, *The LEGO Batman Movie*, *Family Guy*, *Stranger Things*, *American Horror Story*, *Downton Abbey*, *Breaking Bad*, *Skins*, *Die Hard*, *The Silence of the Lambs*, *Trainspotting* . . . and more!

JOHANN SEBASTIAN BACH CREATED SOME OF THE MOST PERFECT, LIFE-CHANGING MUSIC THE WORLD HAS EVER KNOWN AND SINGLE-HANDEDLY ALTERED THE COURSE OF MUSICAL HISTORY.

Think about that for a moment. And then ask yourself what you've done today. . . .

Relax. I'm kidding. It doesn't matter what you've done today. It's just that sometimes classical music is seen as ancient or irrelevant, and Bach proves that isn't true. I want you to hear and learn about this stuff so you can decide for yourself if it's rubbish or not.

Although he suffered a huge number of losses, Bach was determined to make something special of his life and dedicated his entire existence to God and to music. He was super-religious and wrote J.J. (short for *Jesu juva*, Latin for "Jesus help me") at the top of his manuscripts, or *Soli Deo gloria* ("glory to God alone") at the end. "It is God who makes the music," he declared (a little bit too often if you ask me).

Bach's life is as inspiring as it is sad. There is no doubt that he was a complex man, blighted by disappointment and loss from an early age. Not only was death everywhere around him, but his education was often interrupted: in his first three years at school, he was absent for 258 half-days because he endured so much bullying from teachers and other kids. And that's in a world without cyberbullies and Twitter trolls.

After his parents died, he was shipped off to live with his elder brother Johann Christoph. The situation soon became stifling—there was little money, not enough room, and limited opportunities. Luckily, his choirmaster saw how talented his young pupil was and arranged a scholarship for him at a good school that was much better at teaching music. Unfortunately, this amazing school was nearly two hundred miles away at a place called Lüneburg, and Bach didn't have the funds to get there. So (according to some historians, anyway) he set off and walked the whole way, then he threw himself into studying.

Walked.
Two hundred miles.
At fourteen!
No Uber, no subway, just (presumably) a half-decent pair of shoes.

He joined the school at the age of fifteen, at least a couple of years younger than many of the other pupils, and his voice and musical skills (especially on keyboard instruments) were so incredible that he quickly earned a reputation as someone extraordinary. Someone with a kind of Baroque X factor.

This is the kind of person Johann Sebastian Bach was. A man who spent a month in prison for quitting a job that didn't allow him the musical freedom he needed. A man who got into fights, drank too much, and generally behaved like Lil Wayne because he was completely obsessed with doing what he loved and what he believed in, no matter how painful life became. He poured his feelings of rage, hurt, betrayal, love, despair, grief, surrender, and, unbelievably, hope into his music on a daily basis.

He reminds us all of the most important thing in life—find a passion, something you're absolutely crazy about, and give it everything you've got. Ronaldo and Neymar did it with soccer. Jay-Z and Beyoncé did it with rap and R&B. Banksy and Vincent van Gogh did it with art. Jane Austen and J. K. Rowling did it with writing. And Bach did it with classical music. By doing so, he changed the world forever and opened the doors to a musical future that would lead to grime, rap, hip-hop, rock . . . in fact, pretty much any genre of music you can think of. I think it's quite fair to say that without Bach, music as we know it simply would not exist. He truly is the Godfather.

"ONCE I UNDERSTOOD BACH'S MUSIC, I WANTED TO BE A CONCERT PIANIST. BACH MADE ME DEDICATE MY LIFE TO MUSIC."

Nina Simone, *one of the greatest jazz singers of all time*

CELLO SUITE NO. 1 IN G MA PRELUDE

Okay, so let me set the backstory to this piece for you. . . . More than one hundred years ago, a thirteen-year-old boy named Pablo was walking around Barcelona, Spain, carrying a cello. The cello was almost as tall as he was, and he struggled through the heat with it on his back. As he rounded a sharp corner in the old port district of the city, he saw the secondhand music shop he'd been looking for. The bell over the door tinkled as he walked in, and, setting his cello down on the floor and breathing a sigh of relief, he looked around the shop in amazement. As far as his eyes could see, every nook, every cranny, was filled with music **scores** and books, and the whole place smelled of old age and history. He didn't have much money, and the little he did have he'd managed to save from doing odd jobs and begging his father for pocket money. Things were more expensive before eBay came to town. But he was determined to spend every penny on his great love — music.

At the back of the shop was a cabinet with a pile of really old scores on it. They looked dusty and undisturbed, almost as if they'd been waiting there for decades. Our boy, whose full name was Pablo Casals,

walked to the cabinet and pulled up a little chair to stand on — the pile was so high he couldn't reach it on his own.

Buried in the middle of the stack was a book with the words *Bach* and *Cello* on the cover. Pablo loved the cello. It felt like he was born holding one, and his cello had been his best friend for as long as he could remember. But he had no idea that the great Bach had written music for the cello on its own. In fact, almost nobody knew. A few people had seen the pieces, but they had dismissed them as studies to use in practice rather than great works of music. Pablo grabbed them, counted out the correct change, and bought them then and there.

He didn't realize it then, but that thirteen-year-old boy was destined to become the greatest cellist who ever lived. And he had just made one of the most important musical discoveries the world had ever seen. Pablo spent twelve years studying the pieces before he felt ready to perform them in public. And when he did, he shared with the world one of music's greatest gifts. These six cello **suites** are now considered to be some of the finest works ever composed.

JOR,

PLAY ▶

Let's listen to Cello Suite no. 1 — a piece of exquisite music written by Bach and performed by Pablo Casals.

THE OPENING OF THE FIRST SUITE IS A WORK OF ABSOLUTE GENIUS. ALL THE NOTES ARE PLAYED ON THEIR OWN, JUST A SOLO CELLO — NO CHORDS, AND NO OTHER INSTRUMENTS ACCOMPANYING IT EITHER.

Bach uses these individual **notes** to build a kind of castle of sound for his listeners. He uses the **rhythm** of the music to create this rocking, undulating quality, almost like that of a small boat cast off into a calm ocean. He slowly builds up the tension and complexity by making our ears hear two or three different musical voices at the same time, even though there is only one line of notes playing. He does this by making certain individual notes stand out (usually ones at the bottom or top of the cello's register) and letting our ears do the rest. Whether we realize it or not, our brains are brilliant at recognizing patterns and emotion in music. And that allows us to hear and experience many different things at the same time. Everyone who listens to this piece will have a different story in their head because music inspires different feelings in all of us. Some stories will be heroic, some will be sad, some will be calm, some angry. Some will be all of these things at once. What's the story you hear? How does this piece make you feel?

GOLDBERG

In 1741, there was a rich count who couldn't sleep. Back then, if you got bored in the middle of the night, you couldn't play video games or hang out online with your friends because, well, it would be 250 years before those things were invented. So, this count (or so the story goes) did what any rich, bored dude would do and employed a musician to play the harpsichord for him while he was up at night. The harpsichord was the forerunner to the piano and, if I'm being honest with you, really nowhere near as good. But it was all they had in those days, so we'll forgive them.

So, the count hires this musician, whose name was Goldberg. To make sure he had a better pet musician than his friends had (it was all the rage for rich people to hire musicians, and this guy had to have the best of everything), the count took Goldberg to see Bach, the most famous composer in Germany, for lessons. At one of these lessons, the count told Bach that he'd like some new pieces for Goldberg to play in the hope of cheering him up a little at 3 a.m.

As a result, Bach composed one of the most extraordinary and powerful pieces of keyboard music ever written. It became known as the Goldberg **Variations**.

The whole piece is over an hour long and covers every emotion known to man: happiness, sadness, despair, hope, anger, joy. There are slow moments that lull us to sleep and crazy fast moments, like musical shots of caffeine, to get us up and out of bed.

But we haven't got all day, so let's just listen to the opening, which Bach called . . .

the Aria

PLAY

VARIATIONS

I've chosen a recording by one of my heroes, Glenn Gould. He was a rock-star **concert** pianist (a hard thing to be) who was on the cover of *Time* magazine, interviewed in *Rolling Stone* magazine, and even featured on *The Simpsons*. He had this annoying habit of humming while he played, which would drive the producers crazy. Even though they tried to remove the noise in post-production, you can still hear it if you listen carefully.

Now, you'll hear your own story when you listen to it, but when I press play and the piano starts, I imagine a kid. He's in a very calm, picturesque place, but he's stressed. He isn't sleeping well. He's too anxious to have much of an appetite. He has piles of homework and everything feels difficult. It's all a bit too much for him, so one afternoon, he's gone somewhere quiet where everything is beautiful and peaceful. A park, not too far away, but far enough from home to feel like it's an escape.

He starts walking along, alone, enjoying the solitude. He's asking himself some pretty important questions: Why can't he be more popular at school, why's he so bad at soccer, why does he have to take exams, and most of all, why can't he just be left alone to do what he wants?

Then, ninety seconds in—which is about halfway through this piece—he starts to get a bit angry thinking about this stuff. Like why should he have to worry about school and homework? Why can't he just enjoy life as a kid? Surely things shouldn't feel this stressful at his age.

And as if by magic, two minutes and seventeen seconds into the piece (that's 2'17 to music buffs), he gets the answer. Both the left hand and the right hand pick up the pace and the music starts to move a bit faster, becoming more optimistic and hopeful as if it is moving towards something good rather than moving away from something troubling. What the music seems to be telling him is he *shouldn't* have to worry about all that stuff. He can absolutely just enjoy being a kid. And he starts to smile, feeling more settled, more confident, calmer.

A new voice comes into his head, friendlier than the usual one filled with anxieties and complaints. "Relax," it says, "it's all going to be fine—don't worry about the little things, enjoy the fun things in life." And he ends up back at his front door ready to do exactly that.

THIS SHORT PIECE OF MUSIC HAS TAKEN THE KID FROM A PLACE OF ANXIETY AND STRESS AND TRANSPORTED HIM TO A PLACE WHERE EVERYTHING FEELS HAPPIER AND MORE MANAGEABLE.

Mozart
THE MAGIC MAN

THE FACTS OF LIFE

FULL NAME

Although we will always know him by just one name (a bit like Prince or Eminem), he was baptized Johannes Chrysostomus Wolfgangus Theophilus Mozart. Wow. Thanks, Dad.

BORN

January 27, 1756, Salzburg, Austria

DIED

December 5, 1791, Vienna, Austria

CAUSE OF DEATH

Mystery illness, possibly rheumatic fever

They said:

"THE MUSIC OF MOZART IS OF SUCH PURITY AND BEAUTY THAT ONE FEELS HE MERELY FOUND IT—THAT IT HAS ALWAYS EXISTED AS PART OF THE INNER BEAUTY OF THE UNIVERSE WAITING TO BE REVEALED."

Super-scientist **Albert Einstein**

He said:

Mozart was obsessed with poop and often wrote letters to friends and family joking about all things scatological. To his cousin he wrote,

"I NOW WISH YOU A GOOD NIGHT, POOP IN YOUR BED WITH ALL YOUR MIGHT."

FAMILY AFFAIRS

Mozart was one of seven children. He was born to Leopold Mozart, a bookbinder's son who became a composer and violinist, and his wife, Anna Maria Pertl. As a young child, Mozart showed incredible musical ability—he began playing the keyboard at three, was composing from the age of five, and was presented in the Habsburg imperial court at age six. His father was the original pushy parent and took Mozart on a concert tour of Europe, where he performed to court audiences as a child prodigy. By the age of twenty-five, he was living in Vienna, where he met his future wife, Constanze Weber. He became popular for his music and for his brilliant piano playing, but struggled to keep money under control and often borrowed from friends. Tragically, at the age of thirty-five, he fell ill with a mystery sickness and died soon afterward.

MUSICAL OUTPUT

Mozart composed his first **opera** at the age of twelve and in his lifetime penned more than six hundred compositions, including forty-one **symphonies**. His most famous compositions include *Eine kleine Nachtmusik, The Magic Flute, The Marriage of Figaro, Don Giovanni*, and the Requiem in D Minor he was still working on at the time of his death.

MOZART IN (OTHER) MUSIC

Kelis ("Like You"), David Bowie ("See Emily Play," written by Pink Floyd), Electric Light Orchestra ("Daytripper"), Massive Attack ("You've Never Had a Dream"), Missy Elliott ("Who You Gonna Call"), and the Beatles ("All You Need Is Love") have all sampled or been inspired by Mozart's music.

IN THE MOVIES

Mozart's music has been used in the soundtracks for *Alien, Vertigo, When Harry Met Sally, Ace Ventura, Daddy Day Care, The Truman Show, Trading Places, Groundhog Day, Out of Africa*, and *The Greatest Showman*.

LARGER THAN LIFE

Mozart himself has even inspired plays, movies, and TV series, including *Amadeus* and *Mozart in the Jungle*.

Mozart. Where to even *begin* with Mozart . . . Well, here's something to think about:

YOU CAN BUY THE COMPLETE COMPOSITIONS OF JOHANNES CHRYSOSTOMUS WOLFGANGUS THEOPHILUS MOZART ON CD. OR, TO BE PRECISE, ON 180 CDS. ONE HUNDRED. AND EIGHTY.

Even at a conservative estimate, that's more than two hundred hours of music. Now bear in mind that he died when he was only thirty-five years old. Assuming he started composing when he was five (which is insane because most kids are barely out of diapers then, but which also happens to be true in Mozart's case—he could write music before he could write words), that still means producing the equivalent of six albums a year, every year, for the rest of his life. Think about that. Imagine Rihanna or Coldplay releasing SIX albums a year. Every year. For thirty years. It's ridiculous.

He wrote twenty-two operas (most are three to four hours long), forty-one symphonies, twenty-seven piano **concertos**, twenty-three **string quartets**, and hundreds of other pieces. All written down by hand. In fact, not only did he compose so many pieces, but he could simply *hear* a piece of music once and then write it down perfectly from memory on paper. He composed his first thirty symphonies by the age of eighteen. Yep. He was one of *those* kids.

But for me, the MOST amazing thing about Mozart is that when you look at the original manuscripts of his compositions, many of them are completely clean—no corrections, crossings out, edits, or changes. He literally heard perfectly finished compositions in his head and put them down on paper as quickly as he could write. Imagine writing anything—an essay, a poem, a book—and not having to delete or change anything! *That* is why I call Mozart the Magic Man.

He also had a disgusting sense of humor. Which is hysterical because when you think about classical music, you don't tend to think of people being funny—it's often thought of as *very* serious. But this staggeringly talented musical genius couldn't help himself from making nonstop jokes about butts and poop and farting. Hilarious.

He earned plenty of money, but one way or another it kept slipping through his fingers, and he died completely broke. He had a crazy family life, too: his dad was a *real* piece of work, dragging little Mozart around Europe as a child and lying about his age to make him seem even more remarkable. Mozart's dad even made him perform for royalty and wealthy people in a kind of weird eighteenth-century version of *Austria's Got Talent* as a desperate attempt to make some money from him. And it worked, too—people couldn't believe the talent that this kid had. A talent that still, today, has the power to astonish. Sometimes I listen to a piece of music composed by Mozart and think *How is that even possible?* The sheer amount of musical material, the number of **melodies** that flowed out of him, the level of genius on display in his music, the technical perfection of it all. It's mind-blowing. Do listen to Mozart—your life will be all the better for it.

"MOZART'S MUSIC IS SO BEAUTIFUL AS TO ENTICE ANGELS DOWN TO EARTH."

Franz Alexander von Kleist, *German poet*

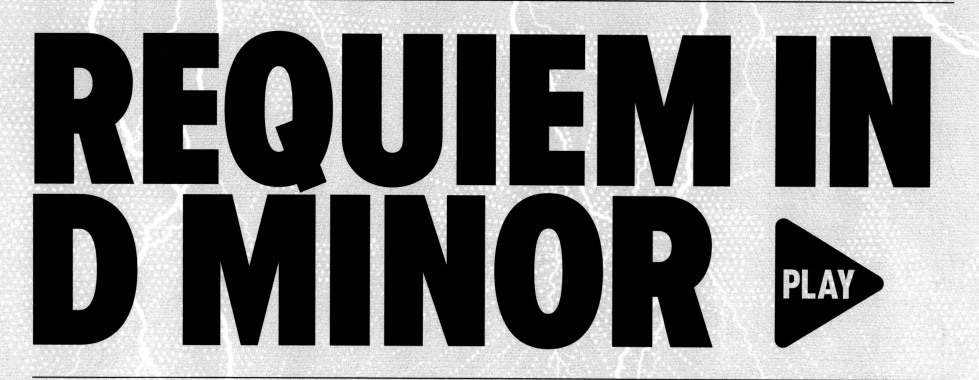

REQUIEM IN D MINOR ▶ PLAY

Mozart didn't know it, but when he composed this piece in 1791, he only had months left to live. He was exhausted, sick, and pretty broke. So when a mysterious "unknown gray stranger" knocked on his door and offered him a ton of cash to compose a requiem (a piece of music played to honor someone who is dead), he was apparently struck by two thoughts:

1) "Ace, that's my money worries sorted out"

but also

2) "Oh God, this is an omen—I'm going to die and I'm composing this requiem for me . . ."

Turns out the stranger was a servant sent by a count who was probably going to pretend it was his own composition and use it to celebrate the life of his dead wife (romantic, if a little bit creepy, huh?).

In fact, Mozart didn't even get to finish composing it before he died; he was two-thirds of the way through when he kicked the bucket, and his pupil, Franz Süssmayr, completed it (really, really well for what it's worth). And what does it matter if Mozart didn't write all of it, anyway? To quote Beethoven . . .

"IF MOZART DID NOT WRITE THE MUSIC, THEN THE MAN WHO WROTE IT WAS A MOZART."

Which is about as good as it gets, praise-wise.

I've chosen part of one **movement** from the whole piece (which has eight movements in total)—the *Dies Irae*, which is a Latin poem written in the thirteenth century. The title means "Day of Wrath," and the poem describes a religious idea called the "Last Judgment," when everyone on earth is sent either to heaven or to hell. It's a happy, light-hearted piece, obviously!

But just listen to the energy of it. From the very first note Mozart grabs our attention in a way that's the musical equivalent of throwing a bucket of ice-cold water over us. The rhythmic pace, the tension, the speed. It almost feels like Mozart won't let us BREATHE for the brief one hundred seconds that the piece lasts. Listen out for the questions and answers in the music, the trumpets and drums pounding away, the violins and cellos furiously rushing around like people being dragged down to hell. There are huge and sudden contrasts from quiet to loud, loud to quiet, and then with a giant bang and all the instruments of the **orchestra** furiously playing, breathless and exhausted, the music ends.

Dies Irae

Turn it up loud and imagine hearing this for the first time in a dark church filled with mourners, a huge, cavernous space with a giant crucifix looming over you, then try to imagine how the listeners must have felt. Like all great pieces of art, it fires our imaginations and takes us on a journey. Here, the inspiration behind the music is what happens when you die, and Mozart is so talented that he manages to both terrify and inspire his listeners at the same time. The way he uses all the instruments of the orchestra and blends the different sounds of the choir and orchestra together, then combines all these different parts into one hundred seconds of pure magic, takes my breath away every time. It's also the reason why, if you say the word *requiem*, musicians will always think of Mozart before any other composer.

HE OWNS IT.

The Marriage of Figaro OVERTURE

Mozart's *The Marriage of Figaro* is now one of the most popular, and most performed, operas in the world. But it almost didn't survive. The emperor of Austria was looking for an opera to be performed in his court (as you did in those days if you were a rich emperor and didn't have Netflix), and this piece was one of many being considered for the job. Apparently, Mozart threatened to set fire to the only manuscript if the emperor didn't choose him, which was quite a risk to take (what a diva). Luckily, though, the emperor had good taste and chose *The Marriage of Figaro,* and Mozart got paid a lot of money for it. Which was excellent news because a) he was broke (again) and b) if he *had* set fire to it, we would have lost one of the greatest operas ever composed.

I know opera has a bad reputation. And I *know* it's a big ask, but I'm going to try to prove to you that it doesn't deserve it.

When this piece was first performed in Vienna, Emperor Joseph II (a VIVP—that's a Very Important Viennese Person) is supposed to have said to Mozart that it was "far too noisy, my dear Mozart. Far too many notes." Which is possibly the stupidest comment ever made in the history of music. This piece is perfection.

The whole opera lasts for three hours. THREE HOURS. So even though I think it is the greatest opera ever composed by anyone in the history of music, ever (is it clear by now that I really, really love it?), for now let's just listen to the opening, known as the **overture** (sometimes also called the sinfonia), which is four minutes long. Much more manageable.

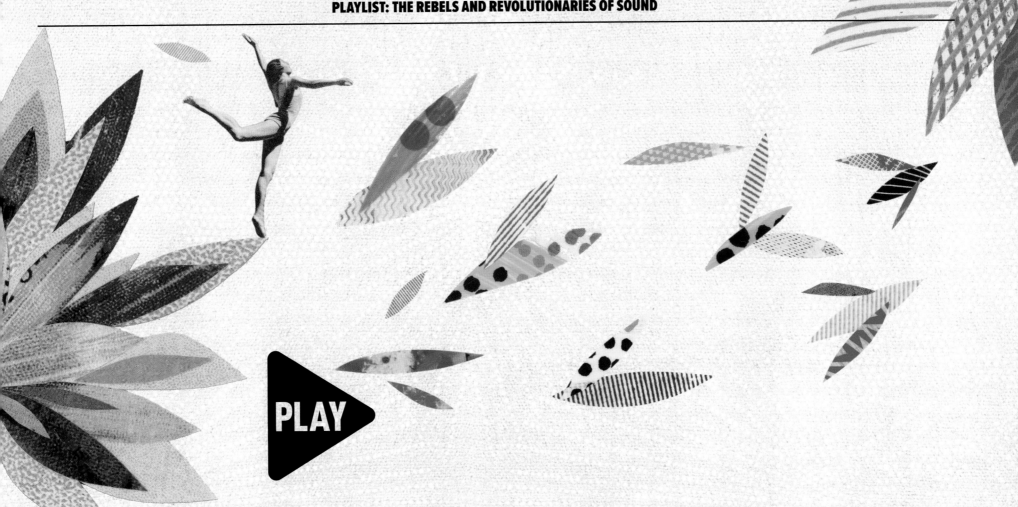

PLAY

As a piece of music, it is furiously difficult to play—super-fast, and trust me, having all the instruments playing perfectly in time together at that speed is *so* tricky, especially when they're playing quietly, too. But because of the speed and the agility of the orchestra, the whole piece just fizzes with energy. Mozart, knowing that you're going to have to sit through hours of his music, grabs your attention right from the start. He begins quick and quiet, forcing your ears to concentrate on the whispering made by the stringed instruments. Then suddenly, with an explosion, the drums, trumpets, and all the rest of the orchestra join in the fanfare.

This overture is like the title sequence to a movie, and so it has to keep its momentum; the worst thing for any composer to see is the audience yawning! It's a whirlwind of **scales** (runs of musical notes going up and down), punchy **chords**, sudden changes in **dynamics** (from quiet to loud and loud to quiet), and movement.

SO. MUCH. MOVEMENT.

And it sets up the rest of the opera perfectly—by the end of the overture, the audience is wide-awake, excited, eager to hear more. Which is great because the story they're about to hear is pretty insane—cases of mistaken identity, women dressed as men, people hiding in closets and jumping out of windows, giant, comic misunderstandings, and on and on in a kind of three-hour soap opera/comedy filled with some of the greatest and most beautiful music ever composed.

THE ORCHESTRA

Simply put, an orchestra is a large group of musicians playing different instruments, usually including those from four of the instrument families: the strings, the woodwinds, the brass, and the percussion. The musicians are seated within their instrument families and next to other musicians who play the same instrument. Each family normally has set positions in the layout of the orchestra, which is shaped like a semicircle.

STRING FAMILY

This section is usually the largest because the string instruments usually make up the basis of a **symphony**. Instruments in this section include the violin, the viola, the cello, and the double bass. The string **instrumentalists** sit at the front of the orchestra, closest to the conductor. Sometimes, a harp or two may also be present, sitting a bit farther back.

WOODWIND FAMILY

The next largest is the woodwind section, and the instrumentalists here sit one or two rows behind the string family. Woodwind instruments include the flute, the oboe, the clarinet, and the bassoon. They each make a very different sound, so the woodwind family can be used in lots of different ways—sometimes they all play together, like a choir, and at other times they pick out a **melody** (the main tune of the piece).

BRASS FAMILY

Sitting behind the woodwind family, the brass family usually consists of the trumpet, the French horn, the trombone, and the tuba. This section is important because it can produce some of the loudest sounds—if you sit next to one of these players, you should definitely wear earplugs!

PERCUSSION FAMILY

The percussion section usually has the widest variety of instruments, including many types of drum, the timpani, the cymbals, the triangle, and the xylophone. These instruments help to maintain the orchestra's rhythm and also give special sound effects when needed (listen to Ravel's *Boléro*—discussed on page 60—to see what I mean!).

THE FACTS OF LIFE

FULL NAME
Ludwig van Beethoven

BORN
Baptized December 17, 1770 (exact birth date unknown), Bonn, Germany

DIED
March 26, 1827, Vienna, Austria

CAUSE OF DEATH
Probably liver damage caused by excessive drinking

STRANGEST HABIT
Forgetting to empty the chamber pot under his piano

They said:

"YOU HEAR THE STRUGGLE IN IT. LOOK AT HIS MANUSCRIPTS, AND THERE'S REAMS OF SCRATCHED-OUT MUSIC THAT HE HATED. HE STOPS AND HE STARTS. I LOVE THAT ABOUT BEETHOVEN, HIS HUMANITY SHOWS IN HIS MUSIC."

Billy Joel, *aka the Piano Man*

FAMILY AFFAIRS
Beethoven was born the eldest of three surviving children. His mother was quiet and melancholic, and his father, a musician at the court of Bonn, was an alcoholic who pushed Beethoven to be a child prodigy, even faking his age to make him seem more impressive, just like Mozart's dad. Despite frequent punishments, Beethoven flourished and at the age of seventeen was sent to Vienna to study with Mozart (although we're not sure if they ever did meet). Then Beethoven's mother died, so he went home again to look after his brothers. They often argued, and not just the usual sibling squabbles. Beethoven fought especially hard with his brother Carl and, when Carl was ill, succeeded in getting custody of Carl's son, Karl, against Carl's wishes (I know—confusing, right?). It was like a nineteenth-century reality TV show. Karl ended up miserable, so desperate that he even attempted to take his own life, and eventually he left what seems to have been a pretty toxic situation.

MUSICAL OUTPUT
One complete opera, nine symphonies, five piano concertos, sixteen string quartets, fifteen string **sonatas**, thirty-two piano sonatas, eleven overtures, hundreds of songs and folk song arrangements—and the list just carries on and on.

IN THE MOVIES
Beethoven's music appears in movies including *The Horse Whisperer, The King's Speech, The Lost World: Jurassic Park, Star Trek: Insurrection, George of the Jungle, Dead Poets Society,* and *Ace Ventura: Pet Detective.*

BEETHOVEN TO YEETHOVEN
In 2016, a symphony orchestra performed a mash-up of works taken from Beethoven and from Kanye West's groundbreaking album *Yeezus*. They called the concert Yeethoven, and it was so well received that they performed a sequel the following year at Lincoln Center in New York City.

It's 1 a.m. and a nine-year-old boy is fast asleep when his drunken father comes barging into his room. The boy is beaten awake and dragged downstairs to a piano, where he is forced to play for his father and his drunken friends for hours. A wrong note results in slaps, punches, and ridicule.

This happens regularly, and even when his father is sober, the boy is mocked, beaten, and forced to practice until he can barely see straight. At age eleven, rather than starve amid this madness (his father spends much of the family's money on drink), he starts to work as an organist.

When he's still a teenager, the boy's mother dies, leaving him and his siblings in such financial hardship that the boy is forced to go to court and wrest control of his father's salary just so the family can eat.

The boy's name was Ludwig van Beethoven.

And despite this unimaginably terrible start in life, he went on to define a whole new style of music and change the musical world forever. Beethoven began composing in the Classical period, but his music was so extraordinary, and so different from anything that had been done before, that it paved the way for something new. A lot of Beethoven's music was about his feelings, about looking within and expressing things he couldn't say—a form of emotional conversation. So his work started to be called "Romantic" music. In fact, in the later nineteenth century, people became obsessed with Beethoven's romantic image: he was the first composer who really captured people's imagination as a brooding genius. Portraits and sculptures of Beethoven looking moody became popular, just as we put up posters of celebrities today.

HIS EFFECT ON MUSIC WAS SO CATACLYSMIC, IT WAS AS IF HE'D SUDDENLY INVENTED A COMPLETELY NEW GENRE.

And he knew it—"There will always be many princes and emperors but there will only ever be one Beethoven," he wrote. Not in arrogance, but in a way that showed his confidence in his own musical genius. Beethoven knew beyond doubt that he was writing for eternity. His confidence in his work was the great solace in his life, and he held on to it with such tenacity because it kept him alive. "To my art I owe the fact that I did not end my life with suicide," he wrote. Bach, Beethoven, and Mozart are without question at the top of my own personal League Table of Composers. But there is one reason alone that puts Beethoven, for me, in top position as the Greatest Composer of All Time, and that is his humanity.

Beethoven really had to struggle and work and fight when he composed. He sweated over each note, working tirelessly on every **theme** to bring it into being. The manuscripts of Bach and Mozart look virtually spotless next to the messy, crossed-out, almost indecipherable madness you find in Beethoven's. While Mozart hurled symphonies onto paper as fast as he could write, with barely any need to correct them, Beethoven stewed and fought and wrestled and raged until he forced what he was looking for out and onto the page. And his music, especially that composed during his last ten years, is unique. He broke the rules with his radical late string quartets, and in his famous Ninth Symphony, when he figured that a whole orchestra wasn't quite grand enough for what he had in mind and decided to bring in a whole bunch of singers, too. He created music like nothing that had been heard before. He's the original rock star.

Beethoven is the most performed, and perhaps the most revered, composer there has ever been. And he was deaf. Yep, that's right. He started losing his hearing in his late twenties. That incredible music he composed? **He couldn't hear most of it.**

He said:

"MUSIC IS LIKE A DREAM. ONE THAT I CANNOT HEAR."

The reasons guessed at for Beethoven's deafness range from typhus and arterial disease to lead poisoning and submerging his head into ice-cold water to keep himself awake.

"EMPEROR" SECOND MO

After an appalling childhood filled with violence and uncertainty, Beethoven also had to deal with his country going to war. In 1809, he was living in Vienna, Austria, under siege—the city was filled with soldiers, and cannons were going off constantly. Even worse, Beethoven's hero, the French emperor Napoleon, the guy he was convinced was going to save the world, had started this war. Beethoven was disgusted. He wrote to a friend, saying "What a destructive, coarse life around me: nothing but drums, cannons, and human misery of all sorts."

But somehow, in the midst of this deadly chaos, Beethoven started to write his "Emperor" Concerto for piano and orchestra. (The name "Emperor" came later, and not from Beethoven himself; for him this was just plain old Piano Concerto no. 5.) This piece is made up of three movements, like a book made up of three big chapters. I want you to listen to the second.

First though, I want you to imagine living in a city filled with soldiers and cannon fire, having survived a hideous childhood, isolated by

deafness and generally in poor health. I want you to think about how that must have felt—to be ill and lonely and scared.

Imagine being at home today with buildings exploding all around you with no warning. Soldiers patrolling the streets and shots being fired. Worrying for the safety of your friends and family. Going to bed and not being sure if you'll wake up next morning. How terrifying must that be? And while you're trying to imagine this scenario, press play.

The movement begins happy and sad all at once. It's in a **major key**, a happy, uplifting **key**, and yet the melody is somehow sad. It sounds a bit like a conversation between two people who are dear friends but discussing some sad news. You can hear violins and cellos. And then after a minute, you think maybe it's ending, as it sounds a bit like a musical conclusion. But it's not the end of the piece; it's just the end of the introduction to the piece. Because, after a short pause, a piano starts to play over the strings. And it is, without a doubt, one of the most beautiful things you'll ever hear. In my mind's eye, as the piano begins, I can see a beautiful bird floating miles above the earth,

ONCERTO VEMENT

PLAY ▶

then soaring down toward the ground and landing on my shoulder. It picks me up and flies away from all the madness and confusion of the world, up to a place where nothing seems to matter. At least, this is what I imagine. I'm sure you will have your own story—it is such a moving piece of music.

As the concerto continues, the piano and the orchestra seem to be having a conversation. They chat back and forth; the piano takes control for some bits, then the orchestra takes over, and then both play and talk at once. They're dancing together and creating something bigger than the sum of their parts. This interlude represents a moment of peace and joy amid all the turmoil Beethoven lived through.

Before Beethoven, most piano concertos were about twenty minutes long (half an hour, tops), but the "Emperor" Concerto lasts forty minutes. It's bigger in every way than any piano concerto that had come before it, and it shook the very foundations of the musical world with its length, its difficulty, and its originality. Beethoven took that feeling of being different and alone and he channeled it into something powerful. He refused to conform to the usual rules and in doing so changed the musical landscape.

IT IS FITTING THAT THIS PIECE IS NOW NICKNAMED THE "EMPEROR" CONCERTO: IT IS TRULY MAGNIFICENT.

"EROICA" SY FIRST MOVE

There are many groundbreaking, significant points in history—moments that changed the world and everything that came afterward. The Battle of Hastings, the First World War, the Holocaust. Mainly to do with war, now that I come to think of it. Which isn't great. But also penicillin, anesthesia, the Great Depression, electricity, cameras, the internet, smartphones, and thousands of other defining changes. There are fewer moments like this in music, but I'd like to tell you about a giant one.

In 1804 Beethoven finished composing a piece of music we now call the "Eroica" Symphony, and in doing so single-handedly reinvented the concept of what a symphony was. The "Eroica" was twice as long as any symphony that had come before it, and totally revolutionary. It was written for an uber-orchestra with more instruments than usual and made technical demands of the musicians playing it that no other composer had ever dared to try. And this was only the beginning. The "Eroica" Symphony marked the start of what became known as Beethoven's "heroic decade," from 1802 to 1812, during which time he also composed the "Emperor" Concerto and began to experiment more and more with musical boundaries. It is no coincidence that this is also about the same time that he became deaf. As Beethoven lost the ability to hear music externally, he had to turn to his inner imagination in order to be able to compose, inventing new and extraordinary things as he did so. When we talk about the history of music, there is *before* the "Eroica" and *after* it.

Have you ever heard a song called "Bohemian Rhapsody"? (If not, WHY NOT?! Go and listen to it now, and be in AWE of Freddie Mercury, the man who wrote it.) In a world of three-minute pop songs, Freddie threw the rule book out the window and wrote an epic song lasting twice that length, fusing different styles and writing crazy lyrics. By doing this, he allowed everyone who followed him to expand their own musical horizons, experiment more, break the rules. That's kind of what Beethoven did here.

HE WAS THE FREDDIE MERCURY OF HIS DAY.

The first movement of the symphony is fifteen minutes long. And right from the very first, very loud chord, it grabs you by the throat and doesn't let go. Audiences had never heard anything like this before—the energy, the volume, the excessive use of the timpani (those loud drums you can hear thirty-nine seconds into the piece), and so on.

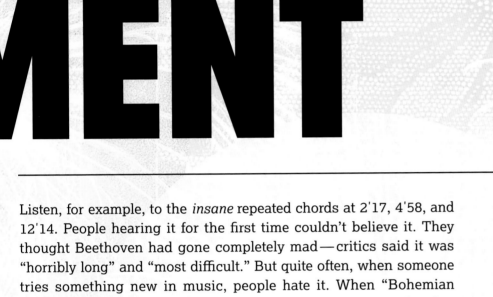

MPHONY
MENT

PLAY ▶

Listen, for example, to the *insane* repeated chords at 2'17, 4'58, and 12'14. People hearing it for the first time couldn't believe it. They thought Beethoven had gone completely mad—critics said it was "horribly long" and "most difficult." But quite often, when someone tries something new in music, people hate it. When "Bohemian Rhapsody" came out in 1975, no one quite knew what to make of it. Now, it's considered one of the Greatest Songs of All Time. Ever.

Anyway, back to Beethoven. He began composing this symphony during a difficult time when his relationships were a disaster, he had realized his deafness was permanent, and he was terrified that he would no longer be able to work. Perhaps this symphony is a response to those thoughts—it's Beethoven fighting back and refusing to give up on life. There are moments of such incredible hope and optimism in this work—12'52 is my favorite bit in the whole symphony. After a long period of loud, crashing excitement, everything just magically calms down and Beethoven takes us on a journey of exploration for a minute or two (although it feels longer) before bringing us back to the music we recognize from earlier in the piece. Only this time it grows and grows, as if he can't stop the momentum he's created, and the music gallops away to the end of the movement. This piece

is so powerful that it really can change your mood and how you're feeling, lifting you up if you're feeling down, bringing you joy if there is sadness.

AND THAT IS THE POWER AND THE MAGIC OF BEETHOVEN.

THE FACTS OF LIFE

FULL NAME

Frédéric François Chopin (originally Fryderyk Franciszek Chopin before he changed it to sound French)

BORN

February 22 or March 1 (depending on who you believe), 1810, Żelazowa Wola, Poland

DIED

October 17, 1849, Paris, France

CAUSE OF DEATH

Tuberculosis . . . maybe. In 2014, his heart—preserved in a jar of alcohol—was investigated by forensic scientists in the dead of night. Their conclusion? That he'd died of tuberculosis . . . maybe.

He said:

"IT IS NOT MY FAULT IF I AM LIKE A MUSHROOM WHICH SEEMS EDIBLE BUT WHICH POISONS YOU IF YOU PICK IT AND TASTE IT, TAKING IT TO BE SOMETHING ELSE."

Charming.

FAMILY AFFAIRS

Frédéric was the second child and only son of Nicolas and Justyna Chopin. At the age of six, Chopin found his first and lasting love— the piano. Passion for the piano ran in the family. His mother was a piano teacher, although it was his older sister, Ludwika, who taught him to play. By the age of sixteen, Chopin was enrolled in the Warsaw Conservatory of Music. Later, he was sent to Vienna for more musical experience, and then he traveled on to Paris. There he met the feminist writer George Sand (her real name was Aurore Dupin) and fell in love. Sand had a strong personality and sometimes wore men's trousers and smoked cigars in public—shocking behavior in 1830s Paris! Their relationship was tumultuous from start to finish, filled with arguments and scandals. Chopin's ongoing tuberculosis steadily worsened, not helped by ill-fated trips to London and the damp atmosphere of Scotland; he died soon afterward in Paris. He was a perfectionist and on his deathbed requested that his unpublished manuscripts be destroyed—fortunately, that request was ignored.

MUSICAL OUTPUT

Chopin wrote more than 230 works in the Romantic style, though only sixty-five of these were published in his lifetime. Audiences would often complain that his piano playing was too quiet for concert halls, but Chopin preferred a quiet, delicate style. His most famous works include the Funeral March from his Piano Sonata no. 2, the dazzling *Fantasie-Impromptu,* and the Nocturne in E-flat Major (op. 9/no. 2).

CHOPIN-TRACKS

Chopin's melodies feature in pop songs from Radiohead ("Exit Music (for a Film)"), Take That ("Could It Be Magic"), Gazebo ("I Like Chopin"), and Alicia Keys ("As I Am").

ON-SCREEN

Chopin's music has been used in the soundtracks for *The Pianist, The Truman Show, Captain Fantastic, Shaun the Sheep, The Simpsons, The Karate Kid,* and *Star Trek.*

CARNIVAL KING

Chopin wrote at least twenty-three **polonaises**, some now lost. Don't know what a polonaise is? It's a Polish dance that's often performed at carnivals. Maybe Chopin was homesick for the country of his birth, which he never saw again after he left it at the age of twenty.

They said:

"HATS OFF, GENTLEMEN, A GENIUS!"

One of the all-time great composers, **Robert Schumann**

Chopin was a musical freak. I'm sorry but there's no other way to describe him. He was born in a tiny, remote village in Poland; he was incredibly shy; and, physically, he was unbelievably weak and underdeveloped. He stood five feet seven inches tall and yet weighed under one hundred pounds. He was so skinny that 97 percent of all other adults alive weighed more than him, and he struggled to grow a beard—at one point he grew a single sideburn on one side of his face! But even now, almost two hundred years after his death, 98 percent of his compositions are still being performed all over the world. In the history of music, there's nobody quite like Chopin.

Sadly, Chopin was not always a pleasant guy. He was spoiled and petulant and acted like a moody child a lot of the time. He liked hanging out only with rich people, spent money like there was no tomorrow even when he didn't have any, and to top it all off, voiced some highly unacceptable views on race. But all of his character flaws aside, Chopin was a musician of staggering genius.

By the age of eleven, Chopin had already been playing in public for four years and was considered a "second Mozart." While still super-young (barely twenty), he wrote, among other things, *both* of his piano concertos, which are still recorded and performed and studied and worshipped around the world as works of absolute brilliance. Even when he was sick (which was most of his life—he suffered from recurring headaches, stomach ailments, bronchitis, laryngitis, and tuberculosis), he couldn't stop composing. He moved from Poland to live in Paris at the age of twenty and never returned home.

He invented or reinvented so many different kinds of piano pieces and, weirdly, only wrote pieces for or including the piano. He didn't write symphonies, operas, or string quartets like pretty much every other famous composer you might care to mention. He was obsessed with the piano, and it became his best friend, his great passion; he spent almost all his time experimenting with it.

Chopin was hopeless in relationships (his one long-term relationship, with Sand, was intensely unhealthy, filled with fights, jealousy, game-playing, and nastiness) and very sickly (even as an adult he would sometimes have to be carried up to bed super-early so that he could sleep), and he died horribly young at just thirty-nine.

HE HATED PERFORMING IN PUBLIC AND IN HIS LIFETIME GAVE ONLY THIRTY CONCERTS.

(To put this in context, I do more concerts than that in a single year!) He much preferred playing private gigs in rich people's houses by candlelight.

When he knew he was dying, Chopin begged his closest friends to make sure that upon his death his heart would be removed and taken back to Poland. After he died, he was buried at the famous Père Lachaise cemetery in Paris, but his friends did as they were asked and smuggled his heart back to Warsaw, where it remains to this day, in the city's Holy Cross Church.

ÉTUDE OP. 10 IN C MAJOR

Until Chopin, exercises for the piano were unbelievably boring. There were scales, **arpeggios**, and really dull and predictable little pieces that made music students everywhere want to scream and punch things.

BUT THEN THIS TWENTY-YEAR-OLD PUNK PIANIST — A REVOLUTIONARY WHO WAS INTENT ON MAKING THE PIANO DO THINGS IT HAD NEVER HAD TO DO BEFORE AND PUSHING IT IN NEW DIRECTIONS — CAME ALONG AND DECIDED TO SHAKE THINGS UP A BIT.

He composed studies for the piano that were not only miniature works of utter genius but also almost unplayably difficult. And I mean ridiculously difficult. Solving-a-Rubik's-Cube-one-handed-underwater-holding-your-breath level of difficult.

Imagine Manchester United training sessions before a game at Old Trafford. The players don't just play matches all day. They break down the areas that need work and practice those specific areas until they're exhausted. Headers, penalties, tackling, passing, and so on. Chopin's piano **études** do the same thing for pianists. He wrote twenty-seven of them—each one designed to work on a specific technical issue.

There are two main problems for a lot of people who play the piano:
1) **Their hands aren't big enough to play all the chords and notes in the score comfortably.**
2) **Their hands get tired too easily.**

Étude op. 10/1 helps with both of those things. It's designed to stretch the right hand and also to train it so that it has the stamina to keep playing. Imagine your right hand stretching as far as it can—each finger really straining and stretching and reaching. Try it now—really stretch each finger as far apart as it can go until all five are beginning to hurt. And then imagine your hand, fingers still wide apart, moving up and down the entire keyboard of a piano, each finger in turn

1

▶ PLAY

pressing down hard and fast, loud and strong, super-quickly. That's what this étude makes you do—it forces you to increase the span of your hand but also to relax it at the same time. Because if you don't relax it, then your hand cramps up or gets too tired to complete the piece. It's so physically challenging that if you don't practice it in the correct way, then you can do irreparable damage to your hand.

This piece reminds me of an enormous waterfall. The notes, like water, cascade and ripple and shoot out of the piano and submerge your ears in a giant wave of sound. There are moments when the notes seem to splash and bounce off rocks, glittering and glimmering, and you can almost hear the sun shining through the water. I first heard this piece when I was really young, and I've never forgotten it. I was super-obsessed with the piano and hearing this (on a cassette tape because I'm old—look it up online) was the first time I listened to something that made my jaw drop and forced me to question how something this difficult was physically possible to play. I would look at the piano score and then look at my tiny hands and think, "No way, it's just not possible." But, life lesson, of course it's possible. It just needed practice and a good teacher. The only annoying thing is that once you've finished learning this one, you can't stop— Chopin wrote another incredible twenty-six études that you will want to learn right away!

NOCTURNE N IN E-FLAT MA

Chopin loved singers. He loved the sound of the human voice and devoted his life to trying to emulate it on the piano. Which is, obviously, hard to do because the piano is little more than a block of wood and metal. Once you press a piano key down, there is nothing you can do to change the sound (you can only make it longer, using the **sustain pedal**). When you're singing, you can make the note louder or quieter, or change the **timbre** to make it throatier or harsher, and lots of other things. But with the piano, that's it—once you've hit the note, you've hit the note and you can't do anything more to change the sound. And so the trick is *how* you hit the note in the first place. You can spend years and years just practicing how to press the piano key down, experimenting with weight and touch and finger strength while knowing no two pianos are the same so it'll always be different when you are playing a new piano! And even then it's very difficult to make the keys of a piano have the same feeling or sound as the human voice.

But of all the pieces Chopin composed, the **nocturnes** are the ones where he comes closest to making this happen. Nocturnes are Romantic pieces for piano, and Chopin's are MAGICAL. He wrote twenty-one of them, and there is almost always a beautiful melody played by the right hand while the left hand plays an **accompaniment**. It's almost like the right hand is the singer and the left is the pianist accompanying her. Although it was an Irish composer called John

Field who invented the nocturne, it was Chopin who made it his own and defined the genre. You've heard of nocturnal animals, which come out only at night; well, as you might have guessed from the name, nocturnes are inspired by nighttime. They're mysterious and dream-like, and while you're listening, you can imagine Chopin sitting at his piano at midnight, setting these intimate pieces down on paper by the light of a candle.

IF THE NOCTURNES WERE PAINTINGS, I THINK THEY'D BE DRAWN IN PASTEL WITH SOFT LINES AND NO HARD EDGES, LIKE A TURNER LANDSCAPE.

There is lots of pedal, a beautiful melody singing out, and an almost **impressionistic** feel to the music, with **harmonies** merging together and creating all of these different sound colors.

0.2 OR

PLAY ▶

The Nocturne no. 2 in E-flat Major is possibly Chopin's most famous composition. Ever since he composed and published it, it has been wildly popular. It feels like a dance to me; I imagine a couple alone at night, a million candles flickering, the moon casting a pale light through the windows as they waltz slowly together. The melody appears right at the beginning. It's repeated three times, each time getting a little bit more complicated and intricate. Here Chopin is emulating the human voice by making the top register of the piano sing, and every time the melody repeats, it feels like the singer is getting more and more confident and wants to make that melody sound even more beautiful by improvising and expanding on it. Sometimes the pianist adds soft, super-fast runs of notes to make it seem even prettier, like a butterfly's wings beating impossibly fast.

And just before the end, something really remarkable happens. Time just seems to stop, and the pianist plays the same four high notes, getting louder and louder, THIRTEEN times in a row before fading away to nothing, ending gently and calmly and quietly—and then finally allowing you to fall asleep.

IT'S PERFECT MIDNIGHT MUSIC. IF YOU'RE WORRIED AND CAN'T SLEEP, LISTENING TO THIS PIECE INSTANTLY MAKES THINGS CALMER AND MORE RELAXED TO ALLOW YOU TO DRIFT OFF. TRY IT AND SEE!

THE TIME LINE OF WES

Music, like painting and literature, has evolved through several distinct stages. Some of these stages overlap, but they are all quite recognizable. Music has grown and developed from medieval chants all the way to today's tracks from the latest bands. No doubt in another fifty years there will be completely new styles of music. . . .

Medieval (c. 400–1400)

In this time, music was most commonly associated with the church, although there was plenty of nonreligious music as well. Much of the music during this period is made up of religious singing and chanting because the church dominated every area of life, and because it was easier to spread music from person to person using voices when **notation** was in its infancy. Early instruments include bagpipes, fiddles and other stringed instruments, shawms (early oboes), and drums.

Baroque (c. 1600–1750)

This period featured well-known composers such as Bach and Vivaldi. It is characterized by extravagant styles of architecture, art, and music: formal but very highly decorated. Opera was pioneered in this period, and musical forms such as the sonata and the concerto also emerged.

EARLY

COMMON PRACTICE

Renaissance (c. 1400–1600)

The French word *Renaissance* means "rebirth," and there was a lot of creativity surrounding music and other arts at this time. Rich people began setting up their own musical organizations to rival that of the church. Singing was still very common, but instead of one line of music being chanted, composers started adding more overlapping layers, woven together like a tapestry. Early keyboard instruments such as the harpsichord were developed.

Classical (c. 1730–1830)

The elaborate style of the Baroque was contrasted with the clear sound of Classicism: instead of ornate lines intricately woven together, we start to hear a clearer sense of melody and accompaniment. Newer instruments, such as the clarinet, come into their own. The period was dominated by the achievements of Mozart, Haydn, and Beethoven, with genres like the symphony and the solo concerto gaining in importance.

ERN CLASSICAL MUSIC

Romantic (c. 1830–1910)

The music in this period was known for its energy and great expressive range, bursting out of the more rigid confines of the Classical style. Beethoven was known as one of the key figures bridging the transition from the Classical period to the Romantic. Other notable figures during this time include Chopin, Schubert, Rachmaninoff, and Wagner. The concept of the virtuoso (an extremely skilled musician) developed during this time: virtuosi were treated like celebrities by audiences who loved to be wowed by their technical feats.

Modern (from c. 1900)

During the twentieth century, advances in technology and communication meant that composers could add together different genres of music—for example, Stravinsky and Ravel incorporated **jazz** into their compositions. In the revolutionary Second Viennese School, composers such as Schoenberg broke down the usual rules of melody and **harmony**. In the 1950s, experimental and **avant-garde** composers brought in electronics and altered conventional instruments (such as "prepared pianos"—all sorts of bits and pieces added on or between the strings—don't try this at home!). An infamous example is John Cage's *4'33"*, in which the musician sits at her instrument for exactly four minutes and thirty-three seconds without making any noise. It's just silence; any sounds heard during that time become the music.

MODERN AND CONTEMPORARY

Impressionist (from c. 1890)

This is more of a style than a separate period of music and refers to a particular "color" or timbre. Impressionist composers were keen to break down old conventions and try out new techniques. As did Impressionist painters such as Monet, composers replaced clear lines with subtle, shimmering textures. The major Impressionist composers include Debussy and Ravel, although neither of them liked the label.

Contemporary (up to the present day)

Contemporary music is as varied as the people who write it. Some of it is **discordant** and jarring and can sound quite strange at first, but open your ears and give it a chance! Some brilliant composers include Elliott Carter, George Benjamin, and Oliver Knussen. John Tavener and Arvo Pärt have written mysterious and hypnotic music that's not too discordant. Then there are film composers, such as John Williams, who specialize in atmospheric scores. And at long last, more women have had the chance to be musically educated in recent times, which means more women are composing, too, including Judith Weir, Sally Beamish, Sofia Gubaidulina, Kaija Saariaho, Unsuk Chin, and many more. . . .

Schupe
THE LITTLE MUSHROOM

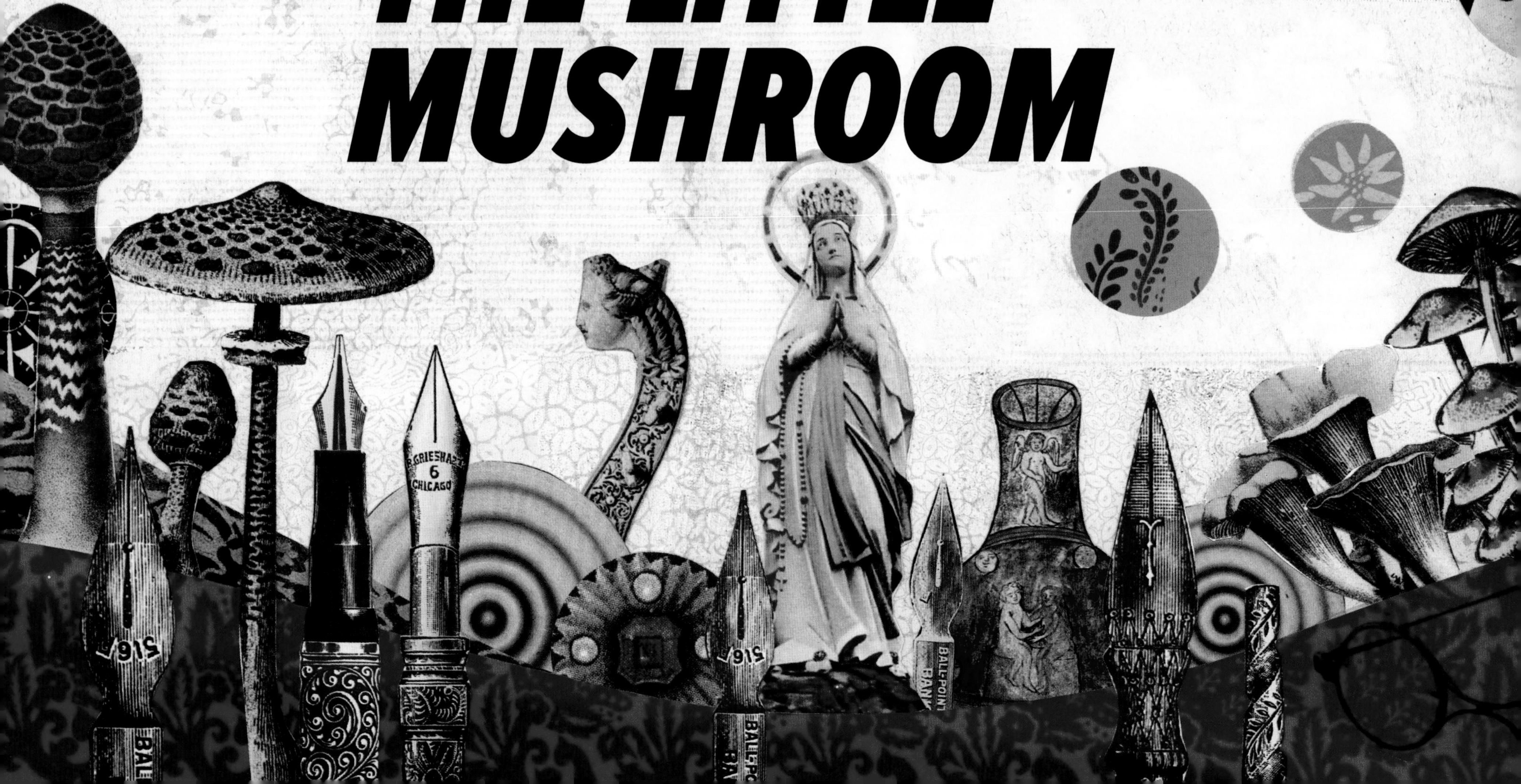

THE FACTS OF LIFE

FULL NAME
Franz Peter Schubert

BORN
January 31, 1797, Himmelpfortgrund (seriously), Austria

DIED
November 19, 1828, Vienna, Austria

CAUSE OF DEATH
The bacterial disease syphilis, though some say that it was typhoid fever or even the treatment for syphilis that killed him. In those days, one of the treatments was to have your whole body smeared in poisonous mercury and to be left in a sealed room. Not nice!

They said:

"WHERE OTHER PEOPLE KEEP DIARIES . . . SCHUBERT SIMPLY KEPT SHEETS OF MUSIC BY HIM AND CONFIDED HIS CHANGING MOODS TO THEM."

Master composer **Robert Schumann**

FAMILY AFFAIRS
Born to a music-loving family with a schoolmaster father who didn't earn very much money, the young Schubert showed musical talent and won a scholarship to a boarding school. He sang and played in the student orchestra—good times. But when his voice broke as a teenage boy, he was forced to give up singing and soon afterward enrolled as a teacher back at his father's school—bad times. When he gained confidence as a composer, he found the courage to leave teaching but still struggled, perhaps because his music was not seen as traditional enough, or because he was too busy composing and having fun to remember to schmooze with patrons who might support his work. He moved to Vienna, and although some of his works were published, fewer than a quarter of them were released in his lifetime. He fell ill and endured a long, difficult decline until his death at the early age of thirty-one.

MUSICAL OUTPUT
During his short life, Schubert penned in the region of 1,500 works. These include more than six hundred songs, as well as more than twenty works for string quartet, twenty-one piano sonatas, nine symphonies, operas, masses, piano trios, and duets. To put that into context, he wrote more than twice as many songs as the Beatles—and there were four of them!

SCHUBERT-TRACKS
It's claimed that the modern three-minute pop song was created by Schubert because so much of his music was composed to be catchy. If you want to hear this in action, listen to "Ave Maria" by Beyoncé, where the singer samples Schubert's own "Ave Maria."

IN THE MOVIES
Schubert's music has been used in the soundtracks for *Minority Report, Peter Rabbit, The Lady in the Van, Dumb and Dumber To, The Avengers, The Twilight Saga: New Moon,* and *Spider-Man 2.*

They said:

"SCHUBERT MAKES YOU WISH YOU COULD PLAY THE MUSIC, RATHER THAN JUST LISTEN."

Wonderful wordsmith **Claire Tomalin**

Franz Schubert was short in stature (only around five feet tall), poor, unappreciated, and sick, but he was an absolute genius. Possibly the most unfortunate composer in history, he was so unusual-looking that the poor guy's nickname was "Little Mushroom." Few of Schubert's compositions were actually published during his lifetime. In fact, he was so poor he often lived in squats, relied on the kindness of acquaintances for food, and was barely able to afford life's necessities. He had a stammer and walked with a shuffle, sometimes slept with his glasses on, wasn't articulate or graceful, and had few close friends. And yet. Oh. My. GOD. The guy may have been short, but he was one of history's musical giants. He composed more than 1,500 works, AND, most incredibly, he died when he was only thirty-one. THIRTY-ONE. Oh, and he was one of FOURTEEN children.

I'm sorry. There are a lot of capital letters in that paragraph. It's just hard not to get overexcited when talking about Schubert. Because he is such an immense inspiration. One of the only composers other than Mozart who could conceive an entire composition in his head and then just write it down on paper, with no need for a piano, he could produce music almost effortlessly and at breakneck speed. He died incredibly young and after a difficult life, but left a legacy that defies belief and that still makes the world's most incredible musical minds sit up in awe. When he was a teenager, Schubert composed more than twenty thousand bars of music in just one year, including nine church works, a symphony, and some 140 songs—including eight in a single day in October 1815!

During his short life, Schubert had some tough times, but there were also some good moments. He became known for hosting a kind of party where he and his close circle of artist, poet, and musician friends would hang out at home, drink wine, play each other's compositions, and provide support and inspiration for one another. The parties became known as *Schubertiaden* and must have been a lovely way to spend a few hours. He also liked to drink. A lot. And could often be found in various pubs getting quietly (or not so quietly) drunk after spending long hours composing.

Sadly the vast majority of his compositions weren't discovered or performed until long after his death. His piano sonatas (all twenty-one of them) weren't even regularly performed until the twentieth century. In the last ten years of his life, he earned today's equivalent of around $9,000 in TOTAL. And when he died, his only earthly possessions were some shabby clothes, a few sticks of furniture, and a sheaf of "old music," valued at about nine pounds, which is less than $1,300 in today's money.

BUT AMONG THE "OLD MUSIC" WAS THE PRICELESS MANUSCRIPT OF HIS NINTH SYMPHONY IN C MAJOR — ONE OF THE MOST MAGNIFICENT ORCHESTRAL COMPOSITIONS IN HISTORY.

You might think I'd choose that symphony to talk about next. But you'd be wrong. Schubert wrote so much ridiculously good music that I've opted for two other pieces instead.

"AVE MARIA"

In 1825, Schubert set to music seven texts from the poem *The Lady of the Lake* by Sir Walter Scott. The sixth of these was called "Ellen's Song III" (the set starts with "Ellen's Song I" and "Ellen's Song II," a bit like a film trilogy). It is the prayer of a girl named Ellen asking for forgiveness for her father's sins as she kneels before an image of the Virgin Mary.

The group (or "cycle") of seven songs proved to be one of Schubert's most financially successful works—he was paid $25 by his publisher for it, equivalent to about $2,500 today, which was a sizeable sum for a musical work at the time. The music was so inspirational to listeners (the songs were wonderful tunes and became instant smash hits) that a traditional Latin prayer was substituted for the lyrics so that it was suitable for use in church. In those days, you knew something was really popular when they wanted to play it in church. And this is why "Ellen's Song III" is now known by its Latin name, "Ave Maria."

OTHER THAN MOZART, I CANNOT THINK OF ANY OTHER COMPOSER WHO HAD SUCH A TALENT FOR WRITING MELODIES, AND IF YOU LISTEN TO "AVE MARIA," YOU WILL QUICKLY UNDERSTAND WHY.

PLAY

The piece goes like this. . . .

There's a simple piano introduction, and then a soprano voice enters with the most sublime tune. It's so uplifting and joyful that it's no wonder that this piece is so often performed at weddings and funerals. I mean, you know you've made it when even Beyoncé samples something you've composed, right?

This piece of music is a perfect example of how something relatively simple can end up being so much greater than the sum of its parts. If you don't know what I mean by that, just sit somewhere where you won't be disturbed. Maybe put headphones on. And hit play. See what happens when you close your eyes and allow yourself to be transported by the music; it's almost as if you're flying. The human voice is such an incredibly pure instrument.

While you're listening to this piece, imagine what it must have been like for Schubert (or anyone having a difficult time emotionally or physically) and see for yourself how the power of this piece of music, although not a cure, can help to make things better. It can inspire us and prove to us that even though life can be difficult at times, there is something bigger and better out there. Whatever magic is contained within "Ave Maria," it goes deeper than words, and deep beneath the words. It tunnels into our hearts and souls in a way that lifts us up and gives us hope.

Music has the power to make us all better human beings, and it can give us the strength to do things that perhaps we couldn't otherwise do. Perhaps that is why poor old Schubert continued to write and work and compose piece after piece of music despite living such a difficult life.

PIANO TRIO
E-FLAT MAJO

One of the final pieces that Schubert composed was this immense piano trio—a piece for piano, violin, and cello. It lasts nearly fifty minutes, which is *enormous* compared to other piano trios. It was published just a few months before he died and, unusually, was performed at a private party in 1828, making it one of the very few late compositions of Schubert's that he heard in his lifetime.

He wrote two full-length piano trios and preferred Piano Trio no. 2 (even if audiences today seem to prefer no. 1). I agree with Schubert. This is, in many ways, his autobiography in musical form. For me it perfectly captures the story of his life through music—with all the ups and downs, the pleasure and the pain.

I've chosen the last movement—it starts quite cheerfully, but at 1'18 there's a second theme filled with repeated notes that changes to a **minor key**, which makes it sound a bit dark and suspicious. This goes on until 2'08, when there are sweeping runs of notes taking turns between all the instruments, and then the whole mood changes again, moving from darkness to optimism and triumph.

This movement is filled with constant shifts in mood that Schubert creates by changing the key, tone, and pace of the piece: moving from happy to sad to uplifting to scary to hesitant to heroic to defiant and on and on. There are so many different melodies—as if Schubert had a constant supply of them that he couldn't help but pour out into the score.

And then he does something amazing. Although we're listening to the last movement, I want you to understand: there are four movements in this piece (remember, each movement is like a chapter in a book), and the slow second movement is incredible—a kind of funeral march, sad and beautiful all at once. Schubert loved the tune from this slow movement so much that (and here's the amazing bit) in this last movement he brings back that theme so the audience has one more chance to listen to it. It starts at 4'49 and it's astonishing because composers hardly ever do this. It seems so out of place. It disrupts the whole movement and makes the audience concentrate even harder. The effect on me is as though I've been reminded of something super-important that I had—until this point—totally forgotten!

O. 2 IN R, FINALE ▶ PLAY

After thirty seconds or so of this slow theme, the movement continues with changing melodies. By this point there are at least four distinct themes weaving in and out of the music, creating a kind of tapestry of dazzling color. Listen out for them at 5'39, 5'55, 6'47, and 7'44 (the original opening theme). How many different tunes can you spot? Sometimes they're alone; sometimes there are two or even three at the same time, piled on top of one another—there are so many ideas, so much ingenuity. In so many ways it's equal to the great Mozart.

Just when you think things can't get any more astonishing, Schubert does it again. For a final breathtaking transformation, right at the end of the piece, he returns again to that slow theme from the second movement. Then with one stunning move from the minor key to the major key (at 12'44), he brings the whole piece to an earth-shattering, heroic close.

It's a master class in composition and one of the greatest works of **chamber music** ever composed. It makes me so happy to think that this is one of the few pieces Schubert wrote that he actually got to hear performed before his death.

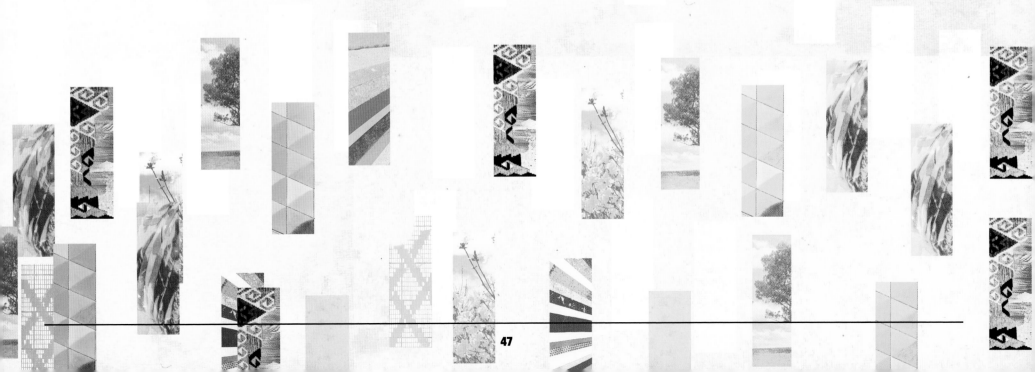

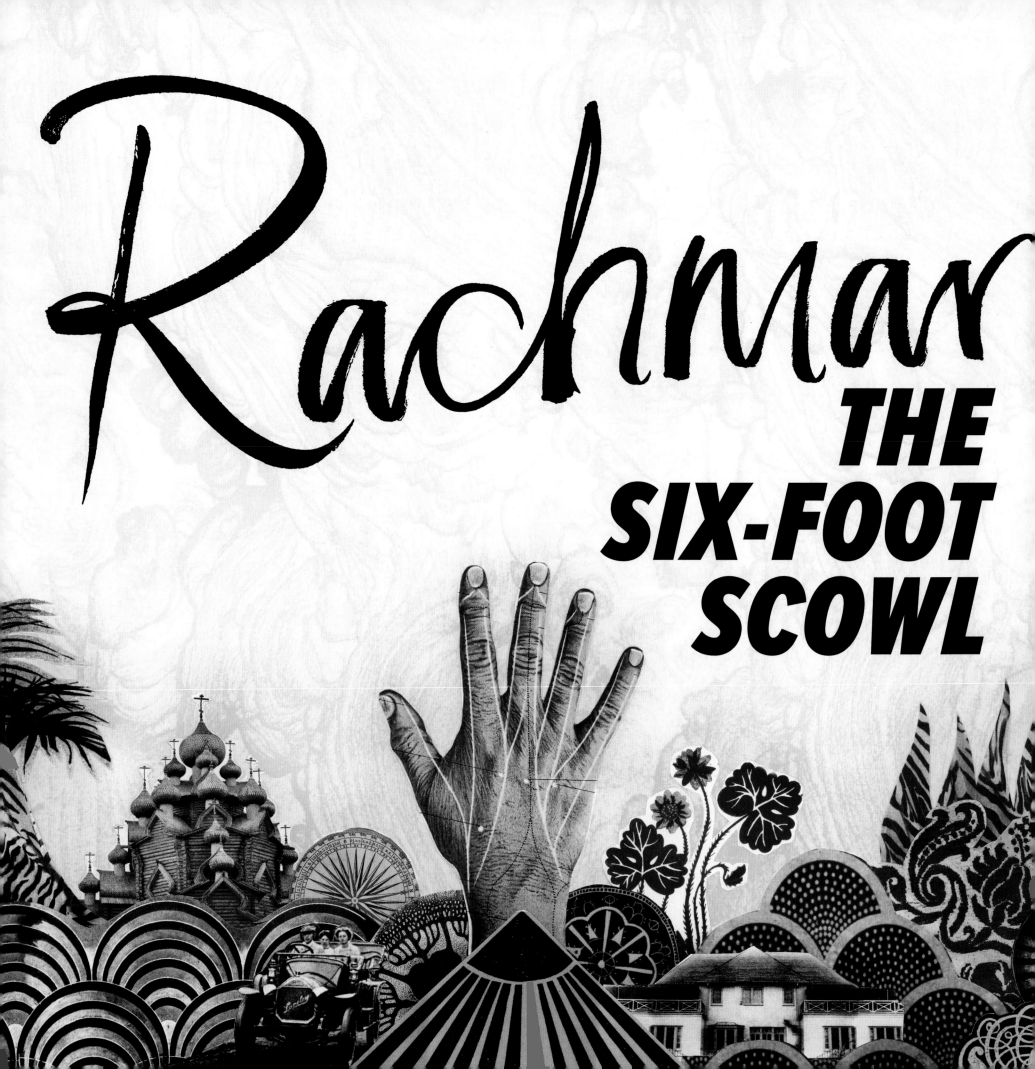

THE FACTS OF LIFE

FULL NAME
Sergei Vasilyevich Rachmaninoff

BORN
March 20, 1873, probably Novgorod Oblast, Russia (nobody is completely certain)

DIED
March 28, 1943, Beverly Hills, California, USA

CAUSE OF DEATH
Melanoma, a very aggressive form of cancer

FAMILY AFFAIRS
Rachmaninoff was born in northern Russia into a landowning family with a long tradition of military service. Unfortunately the family's fortunes reduced over the years, and there wasn't enough money to send young Sergei and his brothers to military school. Instead nine-year-old Sergei, already a talented pianist, was enrolled at the Moscow Conservatory.

SCHOOL DAYS
In those early days, Sergei had the talent but no application. He hated to practice, and hid his bad grades from his mother by altering his school report cards! Despite this, Sergei was lucky enough to be taken on as a pupil by Conservatory professor Nikolai Zverev, regarded as the best piano teacher in Russia at the time.

EARLY ACHIEVEMENTS
Under Zverev's strict guidance, Rachmaninoff transformed into a hard-working, brilliant student. He took his final exams a year early and won the Conservatory's Great Gold Medal—only awarded twice before—and his student opera *Aleko* (which won him the award) was performed at the Bolshoi Theatre in Moscow.

DOWNS AND UPS
Then things started to go wrong. Rachmaninoff's First Symphony, performed for the first time on March 27, 1897 in Saint Petersburg, was disliked by both audiences and critics. It wasn't helped by the fact that the conductor was underprepared and did an appalling job. The composer went into a deep depression and didn't write again for three years, by which time he had taken a course of hypnotherapy. It must have worked—his next piece was the masterful Piano Concerto no. 2.

ON THE MOVE
For years Rachmaninoff lived the life of a touring pianist. When the First World War and then the Russian Revolution in 1917 put an end to foreign travel for most, the composer managed to escape Russia with his family, first to Sweden and Denmark, and eventually to the United States. In the USA, Rachmaninoff spent most of the 1920s and 1930s performing around the country and composed relatively little.

FAMOUS FANS
Singer Frank Sinatra reworked the Piano Concerto No. 2 for his own song "Full Moon and Empty Arms." And anyone who has seen *Bridget Jones's Diary* will also remember Eric Carmen's teary singalong "All By Myself," based on the same concerto.

ON-SCREEN
Clint Eastwood's *Hereafter* and cult movie *Brief Encounter* use Rachmaninoff's Piano Concerto no. 2, too. A lot. It was also featured in the TV shows *Pretty Little Liars* and *One Tree Hill*.

DID YOU KNOW
Rachmaninoff had hands like a Premier League goalkeeper? Yes, really—he could span twelve piano keys with each hand, and many pianists attempting the Piano Concerto no. 2 have wished for longer fingers.

He said:

"MUSIC IS ENOUGH FOR A LIFETIME, BUT A LIFETIME IS NOT ENOUGH FOR MUSIC."

Sergei Rachmaninoff was a giant. He was easily more than six feet tall and his hands were absolutely enormous. Because of this, he wrote ridiculously difficult piano music; he didn't understand (or care?) that most other human beings don't have hands the size of tennis rackets.

He suffered from depression throughout his life, which is why he was referred to by Stravinsky, unkindly I think, as a "six-and-a-half-foot scowl." At a time when his contemporaries were pushing harmonies and tonalities to extremes (by this I mean making music that sounded a little bit weird and very, very different from anything that had come before it), Rachmaninoff saw himself as the last Romantic composer. It was once said of Rachmaninoff that he wanted to create music filled with "flowing, lush effects and illuminated vistas viewed from a romantic point." I think this person meant that Rachmaninoff wanted his music to be ultra-romantic, filled with beautiful melodies, to encompass the listener in warmth, and to transport him or her to an ideal planet. . . .

Which is *exactly* what music should do. Am I right?

As well as being a brilliant composer, Rachmaninoff was a sensational pianist. He became famous at the age of eighteen when he composed and performed his first piano concerto. But a few years later, his first symphony was a complete and utter disaster. The conductor was drunk (which didn't help), and one critic and fellow composer said, "It would be admired by the inmates of a music conservatory in hell."

HAPPILY, HIS SECOND SYMPHONY WAS A MASSIVE, EPIC, PHENOMENAL SUCCESS, AND HE WENT ON TO BECOME ONE OF THE RICHEST, MOST SUCCESSFUL AND CELEBRATED PIANISTS AND COMPOSERS IN THE WORLD.

This happened largely because Rachmaninoff fled his homeland in 1917 after the Russian Revolution and ended up living in the United States. He made so much money there that he built a house in Los Angeles that was an exact replica of his home in Moscow. He loved fast cars and speedboats and ice-cream sodas and generally behaved like a bit of a rock star.

In 1954, eleven years after Rachmaninoff died, *The Grove Dictionary of Music* (a super-influential and very serious musical publication) wrote that the "enormous popular success some of Rachmaninoff's works had in his lifetime is not likely to last, and musicians never regarded them with much favor." It could not have been more wrong. Today he is one of the most popular composers in musical history.

So if anyone has the cheek to tell you that you can't do something you really love, or that you won't amount to much or succeed in life, think about how mean people were about Sergei Rachmaninoff. And how wrong they were. Whatever you dream of doing, go do it. You might just be amazed at what happens. . . .

PIANO CONC IN C MINOR,

After the disastrous premiere of his First Symphony, Rachmaninoff fell into a deep depression that lasted almost three years. During that time he hardly composed a note. He tried many different things to help himself, even visiting the great Russian novelist Leo Tolstoy, whom he hoped would provide some inspiration. ("You must work," Tolstoy told him, ever so helpfully. "I work every day," he replied.) Perhaps Tolstoy was not as inspiring as Rachmaninoff was hoping?

But in 1900, Rachmaninoff saw a hypnotist named Dr. Nikolai Dahl and, somewhat miraculously, began to recover rapidly. One of the first pieces of music he composed following his hypnosis treatment was his Piano Concerto no. 2. This piece became, and still is today, his most famous and celebrated composition. "You will begin your concerto . . . it will be excellent," was one of the mantras Dr. Dahl made him repeat. And, boy, did it work. Despite having a panic attack five days before the premiere, having a cold, and drinking a lot of mulled wine before performing the piece, Rachmaninoff played it wonderfully and it was an enormous success. The audience went nuts.

RTO NO. 2
INALE

PLAY ▶

IT IS ARGUABLY THE MOST FAMOUS PIANO CONCERTO EVER COMPOSED.

It was the soundtrack to one of the best romantic movies ever made—David Lean's *Brief Encounter*. And if you've listened to Muse's breakout album, *Origin of Symmetry*, the concerto should sound familiar—they sampled it on "Space Dementia." (The lead singer, Matt Bellamy, is a classically trained pianist, and he LOVES Rachmaninoff.)

As we know, Rachmaninoff was a giant, and this concerto requires really, really big hands. He asks the pianist to play enormous chords and super-fast runs of notes and jumps from the bottom of the keyboard to the top and back again. The last movement, which we're going to focus on here, is my favorite, for reasons that will become obvious as soon as you listen to it. It has everything that any music fan could ever want—incredible, unforgettable melodies, insane piano pyrotechnics (I mean just *listen* to the first time the piano enters!), excitement, melancholy, heartbreak, and heroism, all in eleven minutes. There are giant cymbal crashes, sweeping romantic tunes with the entire orchestra and solo piano playing at full volume, and an electrifying ending. But it's the big tune, perhaps his most famous melody, that really does it for me. It starts at 1'47, and Rachmaninoff, knowing how special it is, repeats it three times during the course of the movement, each time adding little touches and making it fresher and more magnificent until the very last time (9'55, OMG), when it becomes this enormous, grand, sweeping melody that has inspired dozens of Hollywood composers and would feel right at home in one of the *Jurassic Park*, *Fantastic Beasts and Where to Find Them*, or *Incredibles* movies.

PRELUDE IN G MINOR

Dr. Dahl's hypnosis really did the trick—in 1901, Rachmaninoff composed not only his second piano concerto, but a suite for two pianos, a cello sonata (one of THE greatest works for cello in history), and this amazing **prelude** in G minor. When he was a teenager, he had written a dark, stormy prelude that became very famous, and this prelude became equally famous. In fact, two years later, he would go on to make this prelude one of a set of ten, and later still, he'd become one of many composers (others include Bach, Chopin, Shostakovich, and Scriabin) who wrote preludes in all twenty-four major and minor keys—even though it doesn't seem like he set out to achieve that in the beginning. For other composers, writing a set of preludes in all the major and minor keys was something of a calling card, kind of like musicians today working with Mark Ronson or Lady Gaga—something all the successful ones should do at some point. For Rachmaninoff it seemed to be more of a happy coincidence.

This prelude starts almost like a military march, with a certain degree of swagger. You can imagine a military drum beating alongside the melody as it begins, not too loudly, but perhaps slightly ominously. It gets louder and louder, with giant chords crashing around, before fading out and allowing another most beautiful melody to emerge, appearing over a bass that rolls and repeats, the left hand moving up and down the keyboard of the piano like waves swashing and receding. This melody repeats while another voice enters in the middle, as if the two of them are having a conversation, pleading with each other. It is so romantic (typical Rachmaninoff). And as that fades away, we start to get back to the opening march-like melody, which begins slowly and quietly and gets louder and louder and faster and faster until we are back at full throttle, the piano becoming more and more intense and the poor pianist sweating more and more as her hands fly all over the keyboard with huge leaps and jumps and chords. And then, rather than end in a blaze of glory as we might expect, Rachmaninoff finishes somewhat cheekily, the music just fading out as the pianist's hands run all the way up to the top of the keyboard, like a butterfly flittering away into the air.

PLAY ▶

SERGEI'S ENORMOUS HANDS ARE REALLY OBVIOUS IN THIS PIECE.

With his left hand alone, Rachmaninoff could play a C-E-flat-G-C-G chord. If you have access to a piano or a keyboard, ask someone to show you just how big that chord is and you'll understand how easy it was for him to play pieces like this; he could stretch the entire length of an 8" × 11" piece of paper between his little finger and thumb while also pressing down notes with his other fingers.

The piece lasts only around four minutes, but it is an incredible, joyous, bombastic four minutes, and when it's played live in concert and you see the pianist's hands flying around everywhere, it is absolutely amazing to watch.

See if you can find a video online of Evgeny Kissin playing this piece as an encore after he gave a concert at the Proms in London, and you'll see what I mean; it's not just his hair that is amazing—check out his hands!

Ravel

SHOCK AND AWE

THE FACTS OF LIFE

FULL NAME
Joseph Maurice Ravel

BORN
March 7, 1875, Ciboure, France

DIED
December 28, 1937, Paris, France

CAUSE OF DEATH
Ravel suffered a head injury when he was traveling in a taxi that had a collision on the streets of Paris. His physical and mental health worsened (he already hadn't been well for a decade), and eventually a physician operated in the hope of finding a brain tumor. There was no tumor, but after the operation Ravel fell into a coma and died eleven days later. Several famous composers attended his funeral, including Stravinsky.

They said:

"I HAD THE DELIGHTFUL EXPERIENCE OF SEEING RAVEL IN A YELLOW DRESSING GOWN AND SCARLET BATHING CAP PLAYING THE THEME OF BOLÉRO WITH ONE FINGER AND SAYING TO ME, 'DON'T YOU THINK THIS TUNE HAS SOMETHING INSISTENT ABOUT IT?'"

Ravel's friend **Gustave Samazeuilh**

FAMILY AFFAIRS
Ravel was born to a Swiss father, an inventor who created a circus machine called the Whirlwind of Death! His mother was from the Basque region (spanning parts of France and Spain), and both parents loved music. The family moved to Paris, and at the age of fourteen Ravel was sent to France's most prestigious music school, the Paris Conservatoire. Noted for his unusual style of composition, he kept entering music competitions—and failing to win them. Ravel had the last laugh though, slowly starting to get more and more successful and well-known. And then at the age of fifty-three, his *Boléro* became a huge success. The composition was so unusual that one French woman described him as a madman—*au fou!* She was wrong. Even today, *Boléro* continues to earn Ravel's estate millions of dollars every year.

MUSICAL OUTPUT
Ravel wrote fewer than one hundred works—a smaller number than all of the other composers in this book. But Ravel was proof that less can be more. He carefully studied each instrument in the orchestra, working hard to perfect each piece of music. He was a fan of dance forms, including the waltz, the minuet, and the bolero—for which he later became famous.

IN THE MOVIES
In the Batman film *The Dark Knight Rises,* Batman dances with Catwoman to the musical accompaniment of Ravel's *Pavane pour une infante défunte.*

RAVEL ON ICE
On Valentine's Day in 1984, British ice-skaters Jayne Torvill and Christopher Dean performed a four-minute routine to Ravel's *Boléro*. It was televised to a rapt worldwide audience of more than twenty-four million people during the Winter Olympics. They won gold, becoming the highest-scoring figure skaters of all time and changing the face of ice-skating for ever—all thanks to Ravel. And a lot of practice.

PUTTING ON MY TOP HAT

Clothes were important to Ravel—really important. Maybe it's because he was a small man, at just over five feet tall. It's said that one concert performance was delayed by half an hour because the soprano soloist had to rush out to find his evening shoes for him. Those must have been some very special shoes!

He said:

"LOOK, THEY SAY I'M DRY AT HEART. THAT'S WRONG. AND YOU KNOW IT. I AM BASQUE. BASQUES FEEL THINGS VIOLENTLY BUT THEY SAY LITTLE ABOUT IT AND ONLY TO A FEW."

Ravel is probably France's greatest composer ever.

He worked incredibly slowly, each note having to be dragged out of him. He was also obsessive when it came to detail, and maybe because of this he created some of the most perfect impressionistic music ever composed. He had little time for anything in his life other than music, but he did manage to find time to dress particularly well—he was a proper dandy. Not the most fun guy in the world to hang out with, I'm guessing. But beautifully dressed.

Ravel tried five times to win France's most prestigious prize for composition, weirdly called the Prix de Rome, but never did, because the teachers on the jury were crazy-biased (one year, only the students of one of the judges made it into the final round). This caused a huge scandal and made Ravel even more famous—the fact that he never won and was once even eliminated early exposed a huge case of favoritism, and the director of the jury ended up resigning.

Then, in 1914, the First World War broke out and Ravel volunteered as a pilot. But he was a small, fragile, older man, so he was tasked with driving vehicles instead of actually fighting. Even so, he was in frequent mortal danger, got terribly ill (he had to have a stomach operation and later got frostbite), and at the same time had to deal with the passing of his beloved mother. Her death, along with what he saw on the battlefield, changed Ravel and his music. Everything he composed after the war seems more somber. It also became more jazzy—by which I mean it was influenced by jazz and **blues**, not designed to induce jazz hands in the audience. Ravel was massively excited about American jazz and spent time hanging out in smoky clubs in Harlem and New Orleans. Classical music had rarely borrowed influences from outside its own genre before, but Ravel incorporated much of his enthusiasm for jazz in his later compositions, frequently including classic blues elements such as **offbeat** rhythms and **slides**.

In 1920, to try to make up for the Prix de Rome scandal, Ravel was offered the Legion of Honor (another prestigious French award), but, in a bit of a huff, he refused it. Instead he focused on composing and began touring, conducting, and playing his own music.

ONE TOUR OF AMERICA GAVE HIM A HUGE, GUARANTEED FEE OF $10,000 (MORE THAN $130,000 IN TODAY'S MONEY) AND A LIMITLESS SUPPLY OF CIGARETTES. (PEOPLE STILL THOUGHT SMOKING WAS GOOD FOR YOU BACK THEN. IDIOTS.)

He became super-famous but was never really that bothered about acclaim—he felt, perhaps quite rightly, that since they had given him such awful reviews earlier in his career, the critics' amazing reviews at this stage meant nothing. One of the most cutting earlier reviews had said he was "all insensitivity, borrowing without hesitation not only technique but the sensitivity of other people." Ouch.

In 1932, while Ravel was riding in a taxi through Paris, he was involved in an accident and suffered a blow to the head. At the time nobody thought much of it, but, sadly, it caused damage to his brain and he was never the same again. He had problems eating and sleeping for months afterward, and his friends noticed issues with his spelling and (in)ability to write down music. He died five years later having written barely another note, although he never stopped planning musical compositions in his head.

Boléro

This weird and wonderful piece is Ravel's most famous work and also one of the last things he composed. Ravel thought most orchestras would refuse to play it because it was so repetitive, but from its first performance it was a sensational success (at least for the most part—one listener said that it was undeniable proof that Ravel had gone quite mad).

It's an extraordinary piece. Ravel develops a single moment in time by writing a sixteen-bar melody and then simply repeating it on a loop from start to finish for around fifteen minutes. Think about that for a minute—think of a short tune you like and then imagine simply repeating it again and again and again. And again. For fifteen minutes. Nonstop. It starts as quietly as possible, and gradually, ever so gradually, over the course of the entire piece, it gets louder and louder and louder until by the end it's played by almost every instrument in the orchestra as emphatically as possible. In fact, here's a visual representation of *Boléro*'s volume as it goes from start to finish:

WHAT AN AWESOME IDEA — TAKE A SIMPLE, BEAUTIFUL MELODY PLAYED OVER A CONSISTENT RHYTHM AND REPEAT IT USING DIFFERENT INSTRUMENTS, GETTING LOUDER AND LOUDER UNTIL IT ERUPTS AT THE END.

PLAY ▶

The melody itself is passed from instrument to instrument seventeen times:

1) flute
2) clarinet
3) bassoon
4) E-flat clarinet
5) oboe d'amore (a slightly fatter oboe with a haunting tone)
6) trumpet and flute
7) tenor saxophone
8) soprano saxophone
9) French horn, piccolos, and celesta
10) oboe, English horn, and clarinet
11) trombone
12) some of the woodwind instruments
13) first violins and some woodwind instruments
14) first and second violins together with some woodwind instruments
15) violins and some of the woodwind instruments
16) a lot of the instruments in the orchestra. And finally . . .
17) most but not all the instruments in the orchestra (with bass drum, cymbal, and tam-tam).

And then for the last few bars, the entire orchestra plays along, with the trombones playing amazing **glissandi** (sliding up and down the range of the instrument as quickly and smoothly as possible).

It took Ravel five months to compose (which for him was pretty fast—remember that he composed extremely slowly and methodically). I think maybe he hated people who played the drums—the snare drum literally doesn't stop playing for the entire piece and plays a gobsmacking 4,050 notes with an endless repeat of the same pattern. The percussionist really needs to concentrate: one mistake and the entire orchestra—and audience—will notice it instantly!

Le Tombeau de Couperin.

Ravel saw some terrible things on the front line during the First World War—he was never quite the same afterward. In fact, although he was too old and weak to fight (he drove trucks to the front instead), Ravel was so close to the action and so involved in the war effort that the first performance of this deeply personal piece had to take place well after the war was over, in 1919. Because as unlikely as it might sound, while he was serving in the army, he was still composing. I like to think that perhaps working on music helped him during such awful times. Between 1914 and 1917, he composed a group of piano pieces called *Le Tombeau de Couperin*. *Tombeau* was a term used to describe a musical work written as a memorial. And Couperin was a French composer from two hundred years earlier whom Ravel very much admired. So, in effect, what Ravel wrote was an homage to a composer he loved and, at the same time, a group of pieces to celebrate the lives of people who had died. Each one of the group of pieces (there are six movements in all) is dedicated to the memory of a friend of Ravel's (or in one case, two brothers) who died in the war.

The movement we're going to focus on is the Toccata—the last movement of the whole group and the climax of the piece. It is insanely difficult to play. There are literally thousands of notes in a movement that lasts less than four minutes, and Ravel doesn't allow the poor pianist to rest for a second. There isn't a single pause or gap in the constant stream of notes, and the position of the hands is an absolute nightmare. I should know: I've played this piece a lot and recorded it, too (in fact, the person playing this piece on the playlist is me—I really hope you like it 😊), and sometimes it feels like my hands are about to break. There are several passages where one hand is physically on top of the other—the left hand on top of the right hand and vice versa, and each hand is playing different notes but on exactly the same part of the piano. At other moments, each hand is playing four or five notes at the same time and jumping from one end of the keyboard to the other in the time it takes to blink an eye. And of course, you have to land in *exactly* the right place or it sounds awful.

It is exhausting, relentless, terrifying, and, toward the end, unbelievably loud and exciting. Sometimes it sounds like a dream, with lots of pedal making the notes sustain and hang in the air, the harmonies making impressionistic colors out of the sound. Other times it sounds like a battering ram, driving the noise against a wall at 70 miles per hour. Ravel is truly the master of shock and awe.

PLAY

TOCCATA

BY THE END OF THE PIECE, IT HAS BUILT TO SUCH AN INTENSE CLIMAX THAT IT FEELS LIKE THE PIANO IS GOING TO BREAK AT ANY MOMENT.

It culminates in a glittering cascade of beautiful noise—having started quietly and delicately, it comes to an end utterly heroically. It is a fitting tribute to the men Ravel knew and loved who died in the Great War.

THE LANGUAGE OF MUSIC

Classical music doesn't need words. That's one of the great magic tricks about it—it brings up feelings and images and emotions without using words. But that doesn't mean it doesn't have a language used to describe it. Here are a few of the important words and phrases associated with classical music that have appeared in this book.

accompaniment: supporting music usually played "underneath" a tune or slightly in the background. The piano is often chosen to accompany a singer or instrument.

aria: an Italian word meaning song or song-like piece of music

arpeggio: a chord where the notes are played one after the other in either ascending or descending order instead of being played at the same time

avant-garde: innovative or ahead of its time

blues: a relaxed but often melancholy style of music that was developed by African Americans in the Deep South at the end of the nineteenth century

chamber music: classical music written for a small group of instruments

chord: a set of two or more notes that are harmonious and played at the same time

composition: an original musical piece

concert: a musical performance usually played to the public

concerto: a composition usually made up of three or four movements for a solo instrument and orchestra (the Baroque concerto could be for groups of instruments)

discordant: full of clashing notes that don't really sound "right" together, breaking the rules of harmony

dynamics: how quiet or loud the music is

étude: meaning "study," a short composition that is difficult and designed for practicing a musical skill

glissando: a rapid slide up and down the range of an instrument. (The plural form is *glissandi*.)

harmony: a combination of notes played together

impressionistic: dreamlike or undefined. It describes music that creates a hazy impression rather than a clear picture.

instrumentalist: a player of a musical instrument.

jazz: a very free style of music that grew out of the blues in the late nineteenth and early twentieth centuries. It often includes improvisation, when musicians make it up as they go along.

key: the group of pitches, or scale, that forms the basis of a music composition. It can also mean an individual part of a piano keyboard.

major key: a key that is in the major mode and usually sounds quite light and happy

melody: a sequence of notes that make up a tune

minor key: a key that is in the minor mode and usually sounds dark and heavy

movement: a section of music. Sonatas, concertos, and symphonies are almost always made up of different movements.

nocturne: a composition that is inspired by the night and quite romantic and dreamlike

notation: the special written language of notes that tells us how a composer would like their music to be played or sung

note: the pitch and duration (length) of a sound and its representation in musical notation (like letters of the alphabet but for music). Many notes make up a piece of music.

offbeat: an unaccented beat, or a term describing music that emphasizes those beats. If you count to four rhythmically, you'll probably notice that the "strong" beats, where we put the most emphasis, are 1 and 3, but an offbeat is where the "weaker" beats land, usually 2 and 4.

opera: a story told through music and words. Think of it as an old-fashioned musical.

orchestra: a large group of musicians who play different instruments together

overture: a piece of music that is played before an opera starts, or sometimes on its own

pitch: how high or low a note sounds

prelude: a short composition that is played alone or to introduce a bigger musical piece

rhythm: the pattern of notes of varying durations and accents in a piece of music

scale: a set of musical notes ordered by pitch or frequency, either going up or down.

score: the notes of a classical music piece written down or printed on paper

slide: a flourish in which a musician smoothly swoops between notes

sonata: a piece of classical music written for one instrument or for one instrument and a piano to be played together. (Baroque sonatas sometimes used bigger groups of instruments.)

string quartet: a combination of four string instruments that is very important in classical music (two violin players, one viola player, and one cellist)

suite: a collection of musical pieces, often dances, that are played one after the other

sustain pedal: the rightmost piano pedal, which makes notes sound (or sustain) for a longer period of time

symphony: a long musical composition written for an orchestra, often in four movements

theme: a recognizable melody or pattern upon which a composition is built

timbre: a characteristic that helps to describe the quality of a sound—for example, a note can be harsh or soft

trio: three different instruments or voices playing together, or a composition written for them

variation: a formal technique where musical material (a "theme") is repeated but embellished or enhanced in different ways

First U.S. edition 2019
First published by Wren & Rook (Great Britain) 2019

Library of Congress Catalog Card Number 2019939254
ISBN 978-1-5362-1214-3

DGF 24 23 22 21 20 19
10 9 8 7 6 5 4 3 2 1

Printed in Foshan City, Guangdong, China

This book was typeset in Lexia and Proxima Nova.
The illustrations were created with collage, photographs, and mixed media.

Candlewick Studio
an imprint of
Candlewick Press
99 Dover Street
Somerville, Massachusetts 02144

www.candlewickstudio.com

Picture acknowledgments: The publisher would like to thank the following for permission to reproduce their pictures: Everett Collection Historical/Alamy Stock Photo pp. ii, 48–49 (Rachmaninoff); Everett Historical/Shutterstock.com pp. ii (Beethoven), 3 (Casals); GL Archive/Alamy Stock Photo pp. ii (Bach), ii, 30–31 (Chopin), 4–5 (head); North Wind Picture Archives/Alamy Stock Photo pp. ii, 12–13 (Mozart), ii, 40–41 (Schubert); The Print Collector/Alamy Stock Photo pp. ii, 56–57 (Ravel); © Dave Brown p. iv (Rhodes); CTK/Alamy Stock Photo p. 3 (Grimaud); Garry Gershoff/Getty Images p. 3 (Wang); Gordon Parks/Getty Images p. 3 (Gould); Jack Robinson/Getty Images p. 3 (Ozawa); Sasha/Getty Images pp. 3, 21 (Snow); Tim Ayers/Alamy Stock Photo p. 3 (Barbican); ZUMA Press, Inc./Alamy Stock Photo p. 3 (Lisitsa); wavebreakmedia/Shutterstock.com pp. 4–5 (arms); exopixel/Shutterstock.com pp. 12–13 (horn); Godong/Alamy Stock Photo pp. 12–13, 14–15 (angels), 62–63 (memorial); Granger Historical Picture Archive/Alamy Stock Photo pp. 12–13 (young Mozart), 42–43 (music), 48–49 (young Rachmaninoff); Bill Bert Photography/Alamy Stock Photo pp. 16–17; Chronicle/Alamy Stock Photo pp. 21 (wheel), 56–57 (instruments); astudio/Shutterstock.com pp. 22–23 (trumpets); Khvost/Shutterstock.com pp. 22–23 (flags); Oxygen64/Shutterstock.com pp. 22–23 (stars); Robcsee/Shutterstock.com pp. 22–23 (hands); travelview/Shutterstock.com pp. 22–23 (Beethoven); IanDagnall Computing/Alamy Stock Photo pp. 30–31 (Sand); Heritage Image Partnership Ltd/Alamy Stock Photo pp. 40–41 (diary); Alfio Scisetti/Shutterstock.com pp. 42–43 (papers); konstantinks/Shutterstock.com pp. 48–49 (church); Lebrecht Music & Arts/Alamy Stock Photo pp. 48–49 (boy Rachmaninoff, car), 56–57 (gold pattern, house); SPUTNIK/Alamy Stock Photo pp. 48–49 (house, teen Rachmaninoff); trikona/Shutterstock.com pp. 48–49 (pattern); Laura Kuhn/Alamy Stock Photo pp. 56–57 (deco pattern); Science History Images/Alamy Stock Photo pp. 56–57 (jazz players)